CHRIST MANIFESTED

Christ Manifested

by John Fletcher

Edited by David R. Smith

New Wine Press

New Wine Press
P.O. Box 17
Chichester PO20 6YB
England

First Impression 1800
Reprinted 1826
Reprinted 1830
Reprinted 1835
Reprinted 1968
Reprinted 1969

This edition New Wine Press 1990
© David R. Smith

ISBN 0 947852 67 0

Contents

Foreword

It is most appropriate that the famous *Letters* of the saintly John Fletcher should be re-published in 1968. For this year happens to be the 200th anniversary of the opening of the Countess of Huntingdon's College at Trevecca, for the training of preachers (later known as Cheshunt College). John Fletcher was the first president of the College, which was opened in 1768 by George Whitefield, who preached several sermons on that occasion.

Fletcher was one of that great and remarkable company of men raised up by God in the eighteenth century in connection with *The Evangelical Awakening*—a company which included George Whitefield, John and Charles Wesley, Daniel Rowlands, Howel Harris and John Cennick.

These men belonged to two main groups, determined chiefly by their views on the subject of Free Will and Sanctification; at times the controversy between them was acute and even bitter. But at the first anniversary of the opening of the college at Trevecca in August 1769, the leaders of both parties were present and took part in the worship, the preaching, and the partaking of the Lord's Supper at a great Communion Service.

What made this possible was their common experience of the grace of God, their doctrine of assurance, but above all—their deep experimental knowledge of the Lord Jesus Christ. This is what made them the men they were, and gave them their evangelistic zeal; and this accounts for the

7

authority which was such a great characteristic of their preaching. This is what brought them together, in spite of their differences.

Nothing is more important than this: and it is the theme of these six letters on *The Spiritual Manifestations of the Son of God*.

They have been so long out of print, and almost impossible to obtain apart from the rare copies of the *Complete Works* of John Fletcher. It is particularly good to have them as a separate volume in this way.

I shall never forget my first reading of these letters and the benediction to my soul that they proved to be. They are undoubtedly a spiritual classic.

At a time like this, when many are preoccupied almost exclusively with questions of ecclesiastical organisation and realignment, and others are in danger of falling into a Corinthian and fanatical interest in spiritual phenomena, and the majority perhaps are just practising formal Christianity, nothing can be more salutary than the message of this book. It points us to the one thing that finally matters, and without which all else is more or less vain. It also points us to the highway to revival—both personal and general.

May God bless it and use it to that end.

D. MARTYN LLOYD-JONES

Introduction

It is unfortunate that the name of John Fletcher is not held in such high honour by Christians today, as it once was; considering that his ministry was exceptional by any standard, and that his writings continued to be used by God for years after his death, he ought to have a place in our regard. Even if it is not true to say, as some have done most readily, that he was the most saintly man who ever lived, a knowledge of his life and some acquaintance with his literary efforts, will not go amiss now.

This particular book was not written by him for mass circulation; he intended it for only one reader—a gentleman friend who was bewildered and who could not obtain proper spiritual help in his local church. The six chapters here presented originally took the form of letters in Mr. Fletcher's own handwriting. It was not until fifteen years after the author's death that these letters, along with many other manuscripts, were gathered into two large volumes and published. The edition from which I have taken this manuscript was published by Messrs. Jones and Company, of Finsbury Square, London, in 1830.

In the churches of our generation, it is not uncommon to hear ministers speak lightly of the miracles of Christ and suggest the lack of need for anything supernatural. A more sensitive awareness of the universe and the challenge of scientific discoveries have combined to blind even the most evangelical of Christians into presuming that the Gospel has old-fashioned limitations. It is even said, in some circles, that a belief in anything which cannot be explained in materialistic terms is but superstition; any mention of *divine supernatural events* is smiled at with cynicism.

This influence has so invaded the Church, and so affected preaching, that the doctrine of the New Birth is correctly expounded in very few places of worship. Emphasis has shifted from a mention of the work which only God can do in the life of a sinner, by regenerating him into the kingdom of Christ, to an appeal that even unconvicted persons should *decide* to put their trust in the Saviour. In other words, it is not popular now to exclaim that men need a miraculous experience in order to be saved; it seems that if one wishes to be an acceptable preacher, he must declare only the importance of the congregation *doing* things—the more humanistic the preacher is, the more popular he is likely to become.

This situation is not new; the Church appears to have suffered many tides of unbelief like this, over the centuries. Although we may think that the challenge is new today, spiced as it is with scientific overtones, the problem is the same basically; truth is being attacked by the forces of logical doubt. This being the case, we must confess that if there is a way to combat such an invasion, it must be— as our Christian forefathers well knew—to state, repeatedly, biblical truth with authority. In due course, even though many years may pass, the scriptural preacher will be vindicated, at last.

The title which the first publishers gave to this short work seemed ungainly for the demands of twentieth century librarians, and so the one on the cover has been selected, after much discussion; it is not in either the past or present tense; it depicts a spiritual event in the life of the believer. It was the opinion of the author, and is also that of myself, that the Lord Jesus Christ has many ways of making Himself known to His followers; some of these —if described in human terms—seem to be more remarkable than others, but all can be considered to be *manifestations*—that is, experiences which affect the spiritual senses. The following chapters seek to prove this opinion, from the Bible.

Spiritualists have made use of the word *manifestation* and frightened some people sufficiently to cause them to have no association with the word. This is sad if we recall that the translators have not hesitated to use it in their endeavours to interpret the ancient Scriptures. The word means *something on display, shown plainly, revealed, uncovered, made visible,* and which *provides evidence for proof.* Just because one group of heretics has misused a word which is well known in christendom, it does not follow that we can no longer lay claim to it. Rather, it seems to me, we ought to take every opportunity to make the correct meaning obvious. Spiritual manifestations have been with us from the beginning; the devil may have his own characteristic activities, but this does not mean that the Lord has ceased to manifest Himself in ways of His choosing. We must put up with satanic counterfeits, but we have no reason—just on the grounds of these evil imitations—to deny the Almighty the opportunity of showing His glory, from time to time, in ways that are acceptable to Him. Angels have not ceased to exist simply because some people have said that they have not seen one. Divine manifestations are real to those who have been favoured with an experience of the same.

John Fletcher interchanged the word *manifestation* with the word *revelation* in such a way that one is forced to the conclusion that these two interesting words were, in his opinion, almost equivalent. Although they stem from different roots, there is—especially if one limits their use to the religious sphere—a close similarity. A *revelation* can be defined as *something which makes known, discloses, divulges, unveils, or reveals knowledge*; the word is clearly akin to *manifestation*, therefore, although there must be times when each is preferable. These English definitions are hardly different from those which apply to the Greek New Testament words originally chosen by the inspired writers. This being the case, I have not altered the author's choice of either one or the other in this new edition; in fact, I have encouraged it by my choice of chapter titles.

Every theologian knows that there are good grounds for denouncing the theory that divine revelation is a continuous experience which enables us to learn more about the nature of God, and His purposes, day-by-day; fanaticism and heresy breed in the fertile soil of such ideas. Also, for similar reasons, it is undesirable to encourage people to think that the canon of Scripture is incomplete and that, therefore, it does not furnish the reader with all the information about his salvation, his edification, and his church, that he needs. It is one thing to say that there is still more light and truth to break forth from God's Word, but quite another thing to state that the Church—or some upstart prophet—can add to the divine revelation already committed to print in the Bible. Although the author pleads for personal experiences of Christ that will enrich the individual soul, he is as anxious as anyone else to uphold the sufficiency of the Scriptures. He does not deride a love of the Bible—no minister ever loved it more than he did; he does exhort the reader to discover Christ in the way that enables Him to come and abide with us, and sup with us.

To meet Christ in an intimate way, in the privacy of one's own room, does not make a fanatic out of a man, it humbles him in the way that John Fletcher indicates in the last chapter. Extremism is caused by egotistical activities in the mind of someone who considers that he knows better than the Scriptures.

If the reader, having ploughed his way through every argument here presented, comes to the last page unmoved —without any desire to voice his own 'amen'—he should ask himself if he is but an unbeliever; however unpleasant a fact this may seem to be, it is likely to be true. The pure spirituality of the author's reasoning, and overwhelming presentation of the biblical case, suggest that his opinion is not at fault. Opposition to such a display of divine truth can only be equated with unbelief, as he makes abundantly clear, despite any statements to the contrary. If a man is 'born-again of the Spirit of God' he is no longer earth-bound and essentially materialistic; he is just as aware of the things of the Lord as he is of the things of man. If they do nothing else, these pages may shake some people, who have only a profession of faith now, into realising that one can *know* Him, whom to know is life everlasting.

The reader will learn, after only a few pages, that John Fletcher was a faithful member (although a protesting one!) of the established church, and that he knew the Book of Common Prayer as well as he knew his Bible. The modern non-conformist may find the regular references to the Church of England a little overpowering. It should be remembered that non-doctrinal ecumenism had not then developed and the liberal theology movement had not yet descended upon the scene when the author wrote these pages. It is possible that he would not have been an Anglican vicar, if he had lived in this century. However, I have no right to presume upon these things, and neither have I any authority to edit another's work in the light of present-day opinions. It would be improper for me to delete any of the references to either the established church or the prayer book since they were all important to the author's theme and argument. If the reader is a non-conformist either in England, or overseas, he should take heart at what he reads, for in this book there is proof that the compilers of the Book of Common Prayer believed in experimental religion of the kind that the author pleads for.

It appears to me that although all Christians should have the ability to recognise and comprehend divine manifestations, they do not all do so to the same degree. This may not only depend on the *understanding* which the Lord gives us on these glorious occasions, but also on the type of persons we are. Some are more sensitive than others, and some are more easily able to discern the presence of divine influences. This must reflect itself in the personal experiences which we have of the Saviour. It was William Guthrie—a famous divine of yesterday—who explained lucidly that although the vast majority of sinners ought to experience a *law-work* in their souls as the Holy Spirit strives with them, before they come to know saving faith, not all pass through this state. There are those who are called from conception, like John the Baptist; those who are brought to Christ in a sovereign way, like Zaccheus; those who leave all behind and follow Christ without reserve, upon hearing a single call from the Master; others who discover salvation—in moments—upon their deathbeds. To make rules in these matters, even though one can see a plain pattern for the vast majority, is to harm the souls of a few. The author of the fascinating thesis now in your hands, does not make the mistake of demanding that all believers have one kind of experience; he only intends to show that Christ seeks to manifest Himself spiritually, to every Christian, in one way or another, sooner or later.

As I have said already, we hear much today of the need for people to *do* things; little is heard from the pulpit of the need which the Christian has to foster the presence of his Lord and to know Christ more and more intimately. One could argue that this is not a bad state of affairs and that, if nothing else, it encourages each believer to be unselfish and outward-looking. However, despite its virtues, this approach does tend to make the believer lose interest in personal prayer communion with Christ. Considering the extent of the biblical teaching upon such a personal relationship, we ought to bemoan the lack of this emphasis in modern preaching. It does not matter how intelligently we approach the things of God, nor what wealth of information we have at our fingertips, there yet remains all the difference in the world between knowing a doctrine and knowing the Person of whom the Bible speaks.

If I had not been lovingly encouraged to edit these six letters of John Fletcher and then compile them into this new book, I would not have attempted it; my awareness of the ministry of the author (to say nothing of his saintly life!) make me unwilling to consider altering anything from his hand. However, in view of the fact that this generation needs such a challenge as this title offers, and since I am indebted to Mr. Fletcher for much past inspiration, I have dared to obey the pressure placed upon me. Although fearful of the task, as I first approached it, I now have a sense of gratitude towards those who thrust this honour my way.

I have altered as little as possible, confining myself—as much as I could—to punctuation and style. Also, I have bent over backwards to express the beloved minister in the way that I believe he would have done today, if he had lived in our generation. I have retained the old-fashioned sentence formation, and have changed words only when I suspected that to leave them would make for confusion.

Throughout, I have presumed that the reader will not need to be told where the many quotations are to be found; the few scriptural references I have given are intended only to save the reader from misunderstanding the point being made. With reluctance, I have broken my silence in one or two places and added necessary footnotes.

I am indebted to the Epworth Press and the Evangelical Library for their help, and to those friends who have read the manuscript in order to provide me with the benefit of their opinions; all of their helpful advice has been used.

I consider that the contents of this slim volume are unique and that they will encourage many seekers to enter into much assurance. If my opinion is correct, the hours which I have spent in translating these chapters—for the sake of modern readers—will not have been wasted.

DAVID RUSHWORTH-SMITH

I The Reality of Manifestations

I am of the firm opinion that the Lord Jesus Christ seeks to manifest Himself to all born-again believers, in this life. Realising, however, that an opening sentence of this kind may come as a complete surprise to the reader, I ask only that you will give me time to explain myself. For, although this belief may be thought, by some, to be based upon mere enthusiasm, I am convinced that—for purposes which are worthy of His wisdom—our Saviour desires to reveal Himself to all of His sincere followers, in a divinely spiritual way, sooner or later.

Not only do I believe that this teaching is true, but also I am sure that it is scriptural, rational, and of the greatest importance. Because of this, I am sitting down to write on this profound subject at some length. By so doing, I shall give you a fair opportunity of seeing my error (if I am wrong), or encouraging you (if I am right) in seeking that which I esteem to be the most invaluable of all blessings—revelations of Christ to one's personal soul, productive of the experimental knowledge of Him, and the present enjoyment of His salvation.

Even as an architect cannot arrange for the design and erection of a palace unless he is first presented with a piece of land to build upon, so I shall not be able to establish my doctrine unless I am allowed to prove the existence of the senses by which our Lord manifests Himself. The kind of revelation which I am contending for is not physical or psychical; it is spiritual. If man is to behold manifestations which are wholly divine, he must be granted spiritual senses. Some will question as to whether there are any senses other than those human ones which are associated with sight, hearing, taste, smell, and touch. That is why, in this first chapter, I shall seek to prove— from the joint testimony of *Scripture*, the *Church*, and *Reason*—that spiritual senses are given to regenerate souls. Further, I hope to prove to you that such senses are, and have been, regularly exercised by Christians in every century.

SCRIPTURAL TESTIMONY

The scriptures inform us that Adam lost the experimental knowledge of God by the Fall. His foolish attempt to hide himself from his Creator, whose eyes are in every place, evidences the total blindness of his understanding. The same veil of unbelief, which hid God from his mind, was drawn over his heart and over all of his spiritual senses. He died the death, the moral spiritual death, in consequence of which the corruptible body sinks into the grave, and the unregenerate soul into hell.

In this deplorable state Adam begat his children. We, like him, are not only void of the life of God, but *alienated from it* through the ignorance that is in us. Therefore, although we are possessed of the same animal and rational life which Adam retained after the commission of his sin, yet we are—by nature—utter strangers to the holiness and bliss he enjoyed in his original state of innocence. Though we have, in common with beasts, bodily organs of sight, hearing, tasting, smelling, and feeling, adapted to outward objects; though we enjoy, in common with devils, the faculty of reasoning upon natural truths, and mathematical propositions, yet we do not understand supernatural and divine things. Notwithstanding all our speculations about them, we can neither see nor taste them truly, unless we are *risen with Christ and taught of God*. We may, indeed, speak and write about them, as the blind may speak of colours, and the deaf dispute of sounds, but it is all guesswork, hearsay, and mere conjecture. The things of the Spirit of God can be discovered only by spiritual internal senses, which are, with regard to the spiritual world, what our external senses are with regard to the material world. They are the only means by which a fellowship between Christ and our souls can be opened and maintained.

The exercise of these senses is peculiar to those who are born of God. They belong to what the apostles call the *new man*, the *inward man*, the *new creature*, the *hidden man* of the heart. In believers, this hidden man is awakened and raised from the dead, by the power of Christ's resurrection. Christ is his life, the Spirit of God is his spirit, prayer (or praise) his breath, holiness his health, and love his element. We read of his hunger and thirst, food and drink, garment and habitation, armour and conflicts, pain and pleasure, fainting and reviving, growing, walking, and working. All this supposes senses, and the more these senses are quickened by God, and exercised by the new-born soul, the clearer and stronger is his perception of divine things.

On the other hand, in unbelievers the inward man is deaf, blind, naked, asleep, and past feeling; yea, dead in trespasses and sins; and of course, as incapable of perceiving spiritual things, as a person in a deep sleep, or a dead man of discovering outward objects. St. Paul's language to him, is 'Awake, thou that sleepest, and arise from the dead, and Christ shall give thee light'. Paul described him as being a *natural man*: one who has no higher life than his parents conveyed to him by natural generation—one who follows the dictates of his own sensual soul, and is neither born of God, nor led by the Spirit of God. 'The natural man' wrote the Apostle 'receiveth not the things of the Spirit of God, for they are foolishness unto him: neither can he know them, because they are spiritually discerned.' He has no sense properly exercised for this kind of discernment, his 'eye hath not seen, nor ear heard, neither have entered into the heart of man, the things which God hath prepared for them that love him.'

The reverse of the natural man is the *spiritual man*, so called because God has revealed spiritual things to him by his Spirit, who is now in him a principle of spiritual and eternal life. 'The spiritual man' wrote the Apostle 'judgeth (that is discerneth) all things, yet he himself is discerned of no man.' The high estate he is in can no more be discerned by the natural man, than the condition of the natural man can be discerned by a brute.

St. Paul not only described the spiritual man, but wrote particularly of his internal, moral senses; he believed that mature believers, by reason of use, have their senses exercised to discern both good and evil.[1] He prayed that the love of the Philippians 'may abound yet more and more in knowledge and in all *sense* or *feeling*.'[2] The Scriptures constantly mention, or allude to, one or other of these spiritual senses; allow me to present some examples:

1. Let us begin with SIGHT: St. Paul prayed that the *eyes* of his converts might be *enlightened*; 'that you might know what is the hope of His calling.' He reminded them that Christ had been 'evidently set forth crucified' *before their eyes*. He assured them, that 'the god of this world *hath blinded the minds* of them which believe not' the gospel, and declared that his commission was to *open the*

[1] Hebrews 5:14—'have their spiritual faculties carefully trained' —Weymouth.

[2] Although the author has freely rendered Philippians 1:9 here, his choice of words is more close to the original than the 1611 version: Editor.

eyes of the Gentiles, 'and to turn them from *darkness to light*.' Abraham *saw* Christ's day, and was glad. Moses persevered, as *seeing* Him who is invisible. David prayed 'Open thou mine *eyes*, that I may behold wondrous things out of thy law.' Our Lord remarked that the heart of unbelievers 'is waxed gross, and their ears are dull of hearing, and their *eyes* they have closed, lest at any time they should see with their *eyes*, and hear with their ears, and should understand with their heart, and should be converted.' He counselled the Laodiceans to 'anoint thine *eyes* with eye-salve, that thou mayest *see*'; He declared that 'the world cannot receive' the Spirit of truth 'because it *seeth* Him not'; that the things which belong to peace are hidden from the *eyes* of an unbeliever; and that the pure in heart 'shall *see* God'. John testified that the man who does evil '*hath not seen* God', and that 'darkness hath *blinded the eyes*' of the man who does not love his brother. The eyes referred to are those with which believers *see* the salvation of God; they are so distinct from those of the body, that when our Lord opened them in Paul's soul, He caused scales to grow over his bodily eyes. Also, no doubt, when Christ gave outward sight to the blind, it was chiefly to convince the world that He is the One who can say to blind sinners 'Receive your sight; see the goodness of the Lord in the land of the living; look unto Me, and be ye saved.'

2. Let us now consider the sense of HEARING. If you do not allow for the possibility of *spiritual hearing*, what do you make of our Lord's repeated caution 'He that hath *ears* to hear, let him hear'? Or what can be the meaning of the following scriptures: 'Hear now this, O foolish people ... which have *ears*, and hear not'; 'Ye stiffnecked and uncircumcised in heart and *ears*'; 'Ye cannot *hear* my word—ye are of your father the devil. . . . He that is of God, heareth God's words: ye therefore *hear* them not,

because ye are not of God'? Can it be supposed that our Lord spake of *outward hearing*, when He said 'The hour cometh, and now is when the dead shall *hear* the voice of the Son of God'; 'My sheep *hear* my voice'; 'every man, therefore, that hath *heard*, and hath learned of the Father, cometh unto me'? Do not all sinners stand spiritually in need of Christ's powerful 'Ephphatha! Be opened!'? Is a man truly converted, if he cannot witness with Isaiah 'the Lord wakeneth mine *ear* to hear as the learned'; or say with the Psalmist 'mine *ears* hast thou opened'? Had not the believers at Ephesus *heard* Christ, and been 'taught of him'?; when St. Paul was caught up into the third heaven, did he not *hear* words unspeakable? And, far from thinking spiritual hearing absurd, or impossible, did Paul not question whether he was not then out of the body? And does not St. John positively declare, that he was *in the spirit*, when he heard Jesus *say* 'I am the first and the last'?

3. The sense of SMELL.[1] How void of meaning are the following passages, if they do not allude to that *sense* which is intended for the reception (what the barrenness of human language compels me to call) *spiritual perfumes*: 'How much better . . . is the *smell* of thine ointments than all spices . . . the *smell* of thy garments is like the smell of Lebanon'; 'All thy garments *smell* of myrrh, and aloes, and cassia'; 'Because of the *savour* of thy good ointments, thy name is as ointment poured forth.'

4. As to the sense of TASTE, if believers have not a spiritual faculty of tasting *divine things*, what delusion must they be under when they read 'His fruit was sweet to my *taste*' or 'how sweet are Thy words unto my *taste*!

[1] The introduction of this point may seem improper to a sensitive modern reader. However, the reality of divine fragrance cannot be denied by those who have had close contacts with the Lord: Editor.

Yea, they are sweeter than honey to my mouth'? On the other hand, how faithfully can they speak in this way, if they have themselves *tasted* the heavenly gift, and the good word of God and, as new born babes, have begun to desire the sincere milk of that Word! Surely, if they *eat* of the flesh of the Son of God, *drink* of His blood, and *taste* that the Lord is gracious, they have a right to testify, that 'His love is better than wine', and to invite those who 'hunger and thirst after righteousness' to '*taste* that the Lord is good', so that they also may be *satisfied* with His goodness and mercy.

5. Last of all, we must not forget FEELING; for if we are more than stoics in religion, if we have but one degree more of devotion than the marble statues which adorn our churches, we should have, I think, some *feeling* of our unworthiness, some *sense* of God's majesty. Christ's tender heart was pierced to atone for, and to remove the hardness of, ours. God has promised to take from us the heart of *stone*, and to give us a heart of *flesh*, a broken and a contrite heart, the sacrifice of which He will not despise. King Josiah was praised because his heart was *tender*. The conversion of the three thousand, on the day of Pentecost, began by their being *pricked* in their hearts. We are directed to *feel* after God, if happily we may find Him. Our Lord Himself is not ashamed to be *touched*, in heaven, with a *feeling* of our infirmities. And Paul intimates that the highest degree of stubbornness and apostacy is to be *past feeling*, and to have our conscience *seared* as with a hot iron.

I hope that you will not attempt to set aside these plain passages by saying that they are unfit to support a doctrine, since they contain only empty metaphors and amount to nothing. This would be pouring the greatest contempt on the intrinsic clarity of the Word of God, the integrity of the sacred writers, and the wisdom of the Holy Spirit who inspired them. Just as certainly as there is a *spiritual life*, there are *senses* which are calculated for the display and enjoyment of it; and these senses exist no more in metaphor than the life which exerts itself by them. Our Lord settled the point when he declared to Nicodemus that no man can *see* the kingdom of God, the kingdom of grace here, and of the glory hereafter, except he first be *born of God*—born of the Spirit; just as no child can see this world, except he be first born of a woman—born of the flesh. To put it another way, a regenerate soul has its spiritual senses opened, and made capable of discerning what belongs to the spiritual world, in the same way that a newly born infant has his natural sense unlocked, and begins to see, hear, and taste what belongs to that material world into which he is entering.

THE CHURCH'S TESTIMONY

These declarations of the Lord, His Prophets and Apostles, need no confirmation. Nevertheless, to shew you that I do not mistake their meaning, I shall add to them the testimony of the *English Church*. She agrees strictly with the Scriptures and also makes frequent mention of spiritual sensations; and as you know, *sensations* necessarily suppose *senses*. For example, in the Book of Common Prayer (in the section for Thanksgivings) we are invited to pray that God will 'give us a *due sense*' of all of His mercies, and above all else for His 'inestimable love in the redemption of the world, by our Lord Jesus Christ.' Also, in the same book (in the Office for the Visitation of the Sick) the sufferer is expected to 'know and *feel* that there is no other Name under heaven' than that of Jesus, whereby he can receive health and salvation. The church affirms in the Communion Service that true penitents '*feel* the burden of their sins intolerable', and in the 17th Article of Religion we are assured that godly persons 'feel in themselves the working of the Spirit of Christ'. Further, in the Book of Homilies it is said that 'the Lord speaks presently to us in the Scriptures, to the great and endless comfort of all that have any feeling of God in them at all'; that 'godly men felt, inwardly, the Holy Ghost inflaming their hearts with the fear and love of God, and that they are miserable wretches, who have no feeling of God within them at all'; that 'if we feel the heavy burden of our sins pressing our souls and torment-ing us with the fear of death, hell, and damnation, we must steadfastly behold Christ crucified, with the eyes of our heart'; and that 'true faith is not in the mouth and outward profession only, but liveth and stirreth in the heart, and if we feel and perceive such a faith in us, we must rejoice'; that 'correction, though painful, bringeth with it a taste of God's goodness'; that 'if, after contrition, we feel our consciences at peace with God, through the remission of our sin, it is God who worketh that great miracle in us'; that 'as this knowledge and feeling is not in ourselves, and, as by ourselves, it is not possible to come by it, the Lord would give us grace to know these things, and feel them in our hearts'; and that 'God would assist us with his Holy Spirit, that we may hearken to the voice of the good Shepherd.'

If these quotations are not sufficient, recall that in the Order for Evening Prayer the Church asks continually that the Lord 'lighten our darkness' and in the Litany she prays to be delivered from all 'blindness of heart'.

If I did not think the testimony of our blessed Refor-mers, founded upon that of the sacred writers, of sufficient weight to turn the scale of your sentiments, I could throw in the declarations of many ancient Divines. Permit me to quote from two or three only: St. Cyril, in the 13th Book of his Treasure, affirms that 'men know that Jesus is the

Lord by the Holy Ghost, in the way that they who *taste* honey know that it is sweet, even by its proper quality.' Dr. Smith of Queen's College, Cambridge, in his Select Discourses, observes—after Plotinus—that 'God is best discerned by an *intellectual touch* from Him.' 'We must' says he '*see with our eyes*, or—to use John's words—we must *hear with our ears*, and our *hands must handle* the Word of Life, for the soul hath its *senses* as well as the body.' And Bishop Hopkins, in his treatise on the New Birth, accounts for the papist denial of the knowledge of salvation by saying 'It is no wonder that they who will not trust their *natural senses* in the doctrine of transubstantiation should not trust their *spiritual ones* in the doctrine of assurance.'

THE TESTIMONY OF REASON

However, instead of proving the point by multiplying quotations, let me intreat you to weigh the following observations in the balance of *Reason*:

1. Do not all intelligent people grant that there is such a thing as *moral sense* in the world, and that to be utterly void of it, is to be altogether unfit for social life? If you had given a friend the greatest proofs of your love, would not he be inexcusable, if he *felt* no gratitude, and had no *sense* of your kindness? Now, if moral sense and feeling are universally allowed, between men in civil life, why should it appear incredible, or irrational, that there should be such a thing between God and man, in the divine life?

2. If *material* objects cannot be perceived by man in his present state, except by means of one or other of his *bodily* senses; by a parity of reason, *spiritual* objects cannot be discovered, but through one or other of the senses which belong to the *inward* man. Since God is Spirit, He cannot be worshipped in *truth*, unless He be known in

spirit. You may as soon imagine how a blind man (by reasoning on what he feels or tastes) can get true ideas of light and colours, as how one who has no spiritual senses opened can (by all his reasoning and guessing) attain an experimental knowledge of the invisible God. Thus, from the joint testimony of Scripture, of our Church, and of Reason, it seems to me that *spiritual senses* are a blessed reality.

I have spent so much time in proving the existence of these senses for two reasons. The first reason is because they are of infinite use in the Christian religion; saving faith cannot continue to exist or act without them. If the biblical definition of faith is correct; if it is 'the substance (or subsistence) of things hoped for, the evidence of things not seen', it must be a principle of spiritual life, more or less, attended with the exercise of these senses; according to the poetic and evangelical lines of Dr. Young:

> 'My heart awake,
> *Feel* the great truths: to *feel* is to be fired,
> And to believe, Lorenzo, is to *feel.*'

Until those who are only merely churchgoers see the necessity of believing in this manner, they will trust in but a refined form of godliness. They may add to the confidence of the antinomians[1] the high profession of the foolish virgins; they may even crown their partial assent to the truths of the gospel with the zeal of pharisees (or the regularity of moralists!), but they still stop short of the *new creation*, the new birth—*the life of God* in the soul of man. In fact, it is worse than this, for they stumble at some of the most important truths of Christianity when they presume that the discoveries which sound believers have of Christ, and of the spiritual world, are the delusions

[1] Antinomians are professing Christians who live as if moral laws are not binding upon them: Editor.

27

of enthusiasm, or extraordinary favours which they can very well do without! So, even whilst they allow the power of godliness in others, nominal churchgoers remain satisfied without experiencing divine blessing themselves.

The second reason why I have spent so much time proving the existence of spiritual senses is because the remaining chapters of this book are based upon a belief in them. If, therefore, you are now as convinced as I am that spiritual senses are opened in every new-born soul, you will be more easily able to believe that Christ can, and does, manifest Himself by that proper means. That being the case, my remaining chapters on divine manifestations will meet with a less prejudiced reader!

II The Revelation of Christ to Believers

I am presuming that it is now as obvious to you, as it is to myself, that spiritual senses not only exist, but also that they are the means of communication used by the Lord when He chooses to reveal Himself to us.

A NEW KNOWLEDGE

Do not mistake me for a fanatical enthusiast; I do not insist, as you must know, upon a manifestation of the voice, body, or blood of our Lord to our external senses. It is true that Pilate heard Christ's voice, the Jews saw His body, the soldiers handled Him, and some of them must have been literally sprinkled with His blood, but this had no spiritual significance—they did not come to know 'God manifest in the flesh'.

Neither think that I hold the view that a knowledge of our Redeemer's doctrine, offices, promises, and performances only (such as any unconverted man can attain, by the force of his understanding and memory) is effectual. All carnal professing Christians and all foolish virgins, by conversing with true believers, by hearing gospel sermons, and by reading evangelical books, may attain to a historical or doctrinal knowledge of Jesus Christ. Their understanding may be informed, but their hearts remain unchanged; acquainted with the letter they continue ignorant of the spirit. Even though boasting of the greatness of

Christ's salvation, they remain altogether unsaved and, although full of talk about what He has done for them, they know nothing of *Christ in them*, the hope of glory.

Much less do I mean, by this teaching, such a representation of our Lord's person and sufferings as the natural man can form in his mind, by the force of a warm imagination. Many, by seeing a striking picture of Jesus bleeding on the cross, or hearing a pathetic discourse on His agony in the garden, are deeply affected and melted into tears. They raise in themselves a lively idea of a great and good man unjustly tortured to death; their soft passions are wrought upon, and pity fills their heaving breasts. However, they remain strangers to the revelation of the Son of God by the Holy Ghost. The murder of Julius Caesar, pathetically described, would have the same effect upon them, as that of the crucifixion of Jesus Christ. A passionate play would touch them as easily as a deep sermon, and much to the same purpose, for in either case their impressions and their tears are generally wiped away together.

Nor must you gain the impression that I am writing of good desires, meltings of heart, victories over particular corruptions, a confidence that the Lord can and will save us, power to stay ourselves on some promises, gleams of joy, rays of comfort, enlivening hopes, touches of love; no, not even foretastes of christian liberty, and the good Word of God. These are the delightful *drawings of the Father*, rather than the powerful *revelation of the Son*. These, like the star that led the wise men for a time, disappeared then appeared again, are helps and encouragements to come to Christ, and are not a divine union with Him by the revelation of Himself.

I can more easily tell you what this revelation is *not*, than what it *is*. The tongues of men and angels need proper words to express the sweetness and glory with which the Son of God visits the soul that cannot rest without Him. This blessing is not to be described, but *enjoyed*. It can be written, not with ink, but only with the Spirit of the living God, not on paper, but in the fleshly tables of the heart. May the Lord Himself explain the mystery, by giving you to eat of the hidden manna; and by bestowing upon you the new name, which no man knows except him who receives it! In the meantime, look closely at the following exposition of this mercy, and—if it seems to you to be agreeable to the teaching of the Word—pray that it may be engraved upon your heart, by the power of the Holy Spirit.

EXPERIMENTAL FAITH

The revelation of Christ, by which an unconverted man becomes a holy and a happy possessor of the faith, is a supernatural, spiritual, experimental manifestation of the spirit, power, and love (and sometimes of the Person) of God, *manifest in the flesh*, whereby He is known and enjoyed in a manner which is altogether new. It is as new as the knowledge that a man has when he first tastes honey and wine, if he had eaten nothing but bread and water previously; such a man, dissatisfied with the most eloquent descriptions of these rich productions of nature now before him, is actually tasting them for himself!

This manifestation is, sooner or later and in a higher or lower degree, vouchsafed to every sincere seeker, through one or more of the *spiritual senses* opened in his soul; it may be in a gradual or an instantaneous way that the manifestation comes, according to God's good pleasure. As soon as the veil of unbelief, covering the human heart, is rent by the power of the Holy Spirit; as soon as the soul has struggled into a living belief in the Word of God; as soon as the door of faith is opened—the Lord Jesus

Christ comes in and reveals Himself as being full of grace and truth. Only then is the tabernacle of God *with man*; His kingdom has come *with power*; righteousness, peace, and joy in the Holy Spirit are spread through the new-born soul; eternal life has begun; heaven has come upon earth; the conscious heir of glory cries *Abba, Father*; and, from blessed experience, he witnesses that he has come to Mount Zion, the heavenly Jerusalem.

If, by God's grace, this general manifestation is improved upon, the effects are glorious: now, the believer's heart, set at liberty from the guilt and dominion of sin, and drawn by the love of Jesus, pants after greater conformity to God's holy will, and mounts up to Him in prayer and praise. His life is a course of cheerful, evangelical obedience, and his most common actions become good works done to the glory of God. If he walks according to his privileges, outward objects entangle him no more. Having found the great I AM, the eternal Lord, he considers all created things to be as mere shadows. Man, the most excellent of all creation appears to him altogether lighter than vanity. In fact, he counts all things but loss, for the excellency of the knowledge of Christ Jesus his Lord, esteeming them but dung, so that he may win Christ and, to the last, be found in Him, not having his own righteousness, but that which is through the faith of Christ; so that by new discoveries of the Lord, he may know Him and the power of His resurrection every day more clearly. In the meantime, he casts his sins and miseries upon Jesus; and in return Jesus bestows His righteousness and happiness upon him. He puts on Christ and becomes a partaker of the divine nature. Thus, they are mutually interested in each other; and, to use Paul's illustration, they are espoused and married. Joined by the double band of redeeming love and saving faith, they are *one Spirit*, even as Adam and Eve—by matrimony—were *one flesh.* 'This is a great mystery' wrote the Apostle, but thanks be to God, it is made manifest to his saints.

If you ask 'How can these things be? Describe to me the particular manner of these manifestations!' I can only reply in the manner of our Lord to Nicodemus: Are you a Christian, and do not know these things? Truly, I say unto you, though we cannot fix the exact mode, and precise manner of the breathing of the Spirit, yet, we speak what we do know and testify to what we have seen. Marvel not, however, if we find it impossible to tell you all the particulars of a divine manifestation. You yourself, though you feel the wind, see its amazing effects, and hear the sound of it, you cannot tell whence it cometh or whither it goeth (much less could you describe it to the satisfaction of someone who had neither heard it nor felt it himself). Many earthly things cannot be conceived by earthly men; the blind, for example, cannot conceive the difference between colours. What wonder is it then if unconverted men do not understand us when we tell them of heavenly things?

Nevertheless, I would—in general—observe that the manner in which the manifestation of the Son of God is vouchsafed, is not the same in all persons, nor in the same person at all times. 'The wind bloweth where it listeth', but the Spirit of the living God is more active than this. His thoughts are not as our thoughts; God dispenses His blessings, not as we expect them, but as it pleases Him. Most commonly, however, the sinner—driven out of all of his refuges—feels an aching void in his soul. Unable to satisfy himself any longer, with the husks of empty vanity, dry morality, and speculative Christianity, and tried with the best form of godliness which is not attended with the power of it, he is brought to spiritual famine, and hungers after heavenly food. Convinced of unbelief, he feels the want of the faith of God's operation. He sees that nothing short of an immediate display of the Lord's arm can bring his soul into the kingdom of God and then fill it with righteousness, peace, and joy in the Holy Ghost. Sometimes, encouraged by lively hopes, he struggles into liberty of heart, and prays with groanings which cannot be uttered; at other times, almost sinking under a burden of guilty fear or stupid unbelief, he is violently tempted to throw away his hope, and go back to Egypt, but an invisible Hand supports him and, far from yielding to the base suggestion, he resumes courage, and determines to follow on to know the Lord or to die seeking Him. Thus he continues wandering up and down in a spiritual wilderness, until the Lord gives him the rest of faith, the subsistence of things hoped for, the evidence of things not seen.

This evidence comes in various ways. Sometimes the *spiritual eye* is opened first, and chiefly (though not only) wrought upon. Then the believer—in a divine, transforming light—discovers God in the man Christ, perceives unspeakable glories in His despised Person, and admires infinite wisdom, power, justice, and mercy, in the blood of the Cross. He reads the scriptures with new eyes; the mysterious book is unsealed, and everywhere it testifies of the One whom his soul now loves. He views (experimentally, as well as doctrinally) the suitableness of the Redeemer's offices, the firmness of His promises, the sufficiency of His righteousness, the preciousness of His atonement, and the completeness of His salvation; he sees and feels the Lord's interest in everything. Thus he beholds, believes, wonders, and adores; sight being the noblest sense, *this sort* of manifestation is generally the brightest.

Perhaps his *spiritual ear* is first opened. If so, that voice which raised the dead, says 'Go in peace, thy sins are forgiven thee', and passes through his waiting soul in power. He knows, by the gracious effect that it is the voice of Him who once said 'Let there be light'. He is sensible of a new creation, and can say, by the testimony of God's Spirit bearing witness with his spirit 'This is the voice of my Beloved'; 'He is mine, and I am His'; 'I have redemption through His blood, even the forgiveness of my sins.' And having been much forgiven, he loves much, and obeys.

Perhaps Christ will manifest Himself to the *spiritual feeling*. By taking the burden of guilt, dejection, and sin, from the heavy-laden soul, and—in its place—by imparting a strong sense of liberty, peace, love, and joy in the Holy Ghost, the Lord makes Himself known. The ransomed sinner, enabled to overcome racking doubts and dull insensibility, now believes with the heart unto righteousness, and makes confession with the mouth unto salvation. 'Surely' he says 'in the Lord I have righteousness and strength; this is the finger of God; this day is salvation come to my soul; none but Jesus could do this for me; the Lord, He is God; He is my Lord and my God.' This manifestation is generally of the least order, being made to a lower sense; therefore great care ought to be taken, not to confuse it with the strong drawings of the Father, to which it is similar. Some babes in Christ, who —like young Samuel—do not yet have their senses properly exercised to know the things freely given to them of God, are often made uneasy on this very account. Nor can they be fully satisfied, until they find that the effects of this manifestation are lasting, or until they obtain clearer ones by means of the nobler senses—the *sight* or *hearing* of the heart.

Although I contend only for those discoveries of Christ which are made by the *internal* senses (because such only are promised to *all*), yet I cannot—without contradicting Scripture—deny that *external senses* have been wrought upon in some saints. When Abraham saw his Saviour's day he was, it seems, allowed to wash His feet with water,[1] as afterwards the penitent harlot did with her tears. Saul, on his way to Damascus, saw Jesus's glory and heard His voice both *externally* and *internally*, whilst they that journeyed with him saw but a light and heard words which they could not distinguish.

Sometimes divine manifestations, though actually internal, have *appeared* to be external to those who were favoured with them. For example, when the Lord called Samuel in Shiloh, the pious youth supposed the call was *outward*, and ran to Eli saying 'thou callest me'. Although real to the lad, it seems that the voice had struck his *spiritual* ear only, because the high priest, who was present, did not hear the words with the young prophet. Also, although Stephen steadfastly *looked up to heaven*, as if he really saw Christ there *with his bodily eyes*, it is plain that he beheld Him only with his eyes of faith, for the roof of the house where the court was held, bounded his outward sight. If Christ had appeared in the room, *so as to be visible to common eyes*, the council of the Jews would have seen Him along with the pious prisoner at the bar.

Hence we learn, first, that the knowledge of spiritual things, received by spiritual senses, is as clear as the knowledge of natural things obtained by bodily senses. And secondly, that one can be unsure sometimes as to whether it is the outward or the inward senses which are concerned in particular revelations; you will remember

[1] Genesis 18:3.

36

that Paul himself could not tell whether the unspeakable words, which he heard in paradise, struck his bodily ears, or only those of his eternal soul. Thirdly, we learn that no stress must be laid upon the external circumstances which have sometimes accompanied the personal revelation of Christ, as though these were of the essence of the revelation. If aged Simeon had been as blind as old Isaac, the internal revelation which he had of Christ would still have made him say, with the same assurance 'Lord, now lettest thou thy servant depart in peace ... for mine eyes have seen thy salvation.' If the Apostle had not been struck to the ground, and if his eyes had not been dazzled by the outward light, his conversion would not have been less real, as long as he was as equally inwardly humbled and enlightened. Finally, if Thomas, regardless of the carnal demonstration he insisted upon, had previously experienced, in his inner man, that Christ is the resurrection and the life, he could have confessed Him, with just as great a consciousness—before that personal manifestation —as when he cried out later 'My Lord and my God'.

III God's Purposes in Manifestations

I now wish to consider *why* the Lord manifests Himself
to the children of men, since this is the next important
point. It is not, as is only too obvious, for the gratification
of men's curiosity, but for purposes worthy of His wisdom.
However, in order to discover what these are, we shall find
it better to place all such divine manifestations in three
general classes: *extraordinary*, *ordinary*, and *mixed*; then
we shall consider the design and use of each class, as
revealed in the Bible.

EXTRAORDINARY MANIFESTATIONS

I am beginning with manifestations of the extraordinary
kind, which means that they are either merely external, or
are vouchsafed to a few persons only on special occasions,
and are by no means essential to salvation.

Some extraordinary manifestations are calculated to
rouse the thoughtless into a consideration of eternal issues.
For example, you will remember that manifestation which
some were favoured with, a little before our Lord's pas-
sion, when as Jesus prayed, there came a voice from
heaven, saying, 'I have both glorified My Name, and will
glorify it again'. The people, therefore, that stood by, and
heard it, said that it thundered; they looked upon the
extraordinary as something common and natural. However, others said 'an angel spoke to Him', recognising the

difference between this and thunder; but Jesus said 'This voice came not because of Me, but for your sakes'.

Other extraordinary manifestations are intended as a last warning to notorious sinners. The terrifying sight which Nebuchadnezzar beheld, in his second dream, of a Holy One coming down from heaven, crying aloud 'Hew down the tree', was of this kind. Likewise, the mysterious hand, which wrote Belshazzar's doom on the wall while he profaned the sacred vessels during his revels, was a last warning.

Some extraordinary manifestations are designed for the protection of God's people, or the destruction and humiliation of their proud enemies. Examples of this might include the story of the humiliation of the armies of Egypt by the Lord; also, when He cast down great stones from heaven upon the armies of the five kings who fought against Israel; or when He manifested His presence in Nebuchadnezzar's furnace, in order to quench the violence of the flame, preserve the three hebrews, and convince the raging tyrant that God's kingdom rules over all.

The design of other extraordinary manifestations is to encourage the children of God in dangerous enterprises; or to direct them in important steps. That one in the life of Joshua, before he began the conquest of Canaan, was of this kind; and that in the life of St. Paul, when the Lord stood by him in the prison informing him that he must bear witness also at Rome.

Some are calculated to appoint some persons to uncommon services and trials, or to the prophetic and ministerial office. In this connection, recall how Noah was commissioned to build the ark, Abraham to offer up Isaac, Moses to deliver Israel, Nathan to reprove David, Balaam to bless Israel, and Jeremiah to preach to the Jews.

Finally, there are those extraordinary manifestations

which are designed to fulfil providential means for the deliverance of the people of God, as with Gideon; or to answer spiritual ends of reproof, instruction, and consolation to the church throughout all ages, as were most of the revelations vouchsafed to the prophets, and those to John.

ORDINARY MANIFESTATIONS

The manifestations essential either to the conversion of sinners, or to the edification of saints, and which the Word of God (and the experiences of Christians) show to be common to all believers in the Church, are of the *ordinary kind*, and their use or design is one of the following:

1. To make God's Word spirit and life, quick and powerful, sharper than any two-edged sword, piercing even to the dividing asunder of the soul and spirit, so that the gospel may not come to sinners in word only, but also in power, and in the Holy Ghost, and in much assurance.

2. To ease an anguished conscience, and impart the peace of God to a troubled mind—as in the case of broken-hearted David, mourning Hezekiah, weeping Peter and Paul agonising in prayer.

3. To reveal Christ to us, and in us, so as to make us believe in a saving way, and to know in whom we have believed, according to the experiences of Peter, Lydia, Cornelius, and every living member of the Body of Christ.

4. To open a blessed fellowship, and keep up a delightful communion, with Christ—as appears from the experiences of believers illustrated in the Canticles.

5. To silence the residue of self-righteousness in us, and to deepen the humiliation of our souls—as in the case of Job. To make us grow in grace, and in the knowledge of our Lord Jesus Christ; to bruise Satan under our feet; to bruise the serpent's head in our hearts; to seal the exceeding great and precious promises given to us, that we might

be partakers of the divine nature, and to continue immovable, always abounding in the work of faith, the patience of hope, and the labour of love. In a word, they strengthen us with might, by God's Spirit, in the inner man, so that Christ may dwell in our hearts by faith, and so that we may be filled with all the fullness of God.

6. To prepare us for great trials, support us under them, and to comfort us after them. This was our Lord's experience before His temptation, after He had overcome the tempter, and when He was at the height of His agony. This was also the situation in the case of David, Paul, and of all the Apostles, when they had been scourged for the name of Jesus; and it is still the case of all true, and deep, mourners of Zion.

7. And lastly, to make us depart in peace, as Simeon did, or to die in perfect love with our enemies, in the full triumph of faith, like Stephen. All who live and die in the Lord, partake—more or less—of these ordinary displays of Christ's powerful presence, and I wish you to remember, that it is *chiefly* (if not only) in support of these important manifestations that I take up my pen.

MIXED MANIFESTATIONS

The third class of manifestations is that of *mixed ones*; so called, because they are partly *extraordinary* and partly *ordinary*. Some are ordinary in their design but extraordinary in their circumstances. The manifestation to the Apostles in Acts 4:31 was like this; the design of it was merely common, that is to comfort them under contempt, and to encourage them both to do good and to suffer evil; however, the shaking of the place where they were assembled was an *uncommon* circumstance. The same may be said of the descent of the Holy Spirit on the 120 disciples who were assembled on the day of Pentecost, and later on

Cornelius and his soldiers. That they should be baptised with the Holy Ghost and spiritual fire was not extraordinary, since it is the common blessing (which can alone make a man a Christian, or confirm him in the faith), but that the sound of a rushing wind should be heard, and luminous appearances seen to be resting upon them, that they should have been enabled to speak the wonderful works of God in other tongues, were *uncommon* circumstances attending their spiritual baptism.

Some manifestations are mixed, both as to their design and circumstances. That the iniquity of Isaiah should be put away, and that Saul should be converted, were not uncommon things—they are the common effects of ordinary manifestations—but that the Prophet should be commissioned to preach to the Jews and that Paul should be called to open the eyes of the Gentiles were extraordinary circumstances; as extraordinary as a flying cherub appearing to the one, and an unusually bright light blinding the other.

BLIND PREJUDICE

For want of distinguishing properly between what is ordinary and extraordinary in mixed manifestations, those people who are not possessed of a clear head (or of an honest heart) often conclude that none but fanatics speak today of divine manifestations! If they hear someone preach that they must be converted in the way that Paul was, they pertly ask if this means that they are Jews, or if they must be struck to the earth by a voice from heaven! Such people wilfully forget that our Lord spoke to His hearers as to sinful men, and not as to bigoted Jews, when He said 'Except ye be converted, ye cannot enter the kingdom of heaven'. They obstinately refuse to see that the circumstances of the Apostle's falling to the ground were not essential to his conversion, and had no other use than to

42

make his call more remarkable for the Jews and of comfort to the Christians. When the same prejudiced persons are told that they must be *born of the Spirit*, and receive the Holy Ghost like Cornelius and his servants, they overlook the ordinary baptism of the Spirit and take hold of the extraordinary circumstances of the gift of tongues, which was imparted for a season in order to remove the prejudices of the Jews and to attract the attention of the Gentiles; with a sneer and a charge of enthusiasm they think that they can overturn the apostolic saying 'If any man have not the Spirit of Christ, he is none of His'. Reader, be not deceived by these persons! Acknowledge that, even as you want the regenerating knowledge of Christ, you want the manifestation of His Spirit, without which He can never be known savingly.

So, although I contend only for the ordinary manifestations of the Lord Jesus Christ, I am far from believing that all *extraordinary* or *mixed* manifestations have ceased. Such a concession would savour too much of the spirit of unbelief which prevails in the church today. These extraordinary manifestations are more frequent than many imagine! To show you how far I am from agreeing with the modern spirit of unbelief, let me say that I am so attached to the Bible, as to say of many who pass for ministers of Christ 'Woe to the foolish prophets, that follow their own spirit, and have *seen nothing*; that say "the Lord says" and yet the Lord hath not sent them.' I think the desire to be styled 'reverend' or 'right reverend', and the prospect of a 'living' or a 'mitre', are very *improper* motives for assuming the sacred office. Am I sufficiently an enthusiast as to believe that the Church is right in requiring that all her ministers should not only be *called*, but also be *moved* by the Holy Ghost, before they take upon themselves the office of Ambassadors for Christ.

43

Having mentioned the *design* and *use* of ordinary manifestations, it may not be improper to touch upon the *abuse* of them. Their genuine tendency is to humble one to the dust. The language of those who are favoured with them, is 'Will God indeed dwell on the earth'; 'Lord, what is man, that Thou art mindful of him, and the son of man, that Thou visitest him'; 'Now that I see thee, I abhor myself: I am not worthy of the least of thy mercies: I am dust and ashes.' But as there is nothing which the heart of man cannot be tempted to corrupt and pervert, so, as soon as the power attending the manifestation is a little abated, Satan begins to shoot his fiery darts of spiritual pride. 'You are a peculiar favourite of heaven' whispers that old serpent 'few are so highly blessed. All your enemies are scattered; you need not be so watchful in prayer, and so strict in self-denial; you shall never fall.' If the believer is not upon his guard and does not quench these fiery darts with his shield as fast as the enemy throws them, he is soon wounded, and pride kindles again in him.

St. Paul himself was in danger from this quarter and so there was given him a thorn in the flesh, a messenger of Satan to buffet him, lest he should be exalted above measure, through the abundance of the revelations. Aaron and Miriam fell into this snare, when they spoke against Moses, saying 'Hath the Lord indeed spoken only by Moses? Hath not He spoken also by us?' David likewise acknowledged his error in this respect: 'In my prosperity I said "I shall never be moved," Thou hast made my mountain to stand strong, but Thou didst hide Thy face from me, and I was troubled.' The way to avoid danger is to recognise it before hand, to look much to the lowly Jesus, and upon the first approach of a temptation towards pride, to give—with double diligence—all the glory to Him who has graciously bestowed all, and to take—with double care—all the shame of our sins to ourselves. Paul's advice in this respect is excellent: 'Because of unbelief some were broken off, and thou standest by faith. Be not high-minded, but fear.'

A genuine effect of divine manifestations is to produce an increase of confidence in the Lord, and of activity in His service. What holy boldness filled the souls of those worthies, who 'through faith subdued kingdoms, wrought righteousness ... and turned to flight the armies of the aliens'? See how the love of Christ constrained the disciples to speak and act for God after the day of Pentecost; nothing could exceed their fortitude and diligence! Nevertheless, if you yield to the temptation to be proud, not only is the Comforter grieved, but carnal security, spiritual sloth, and indulgence of the flesh, prevail. The deluded Christian fancies himself to be the same still, though shorn of his strength, like Samson. 'Soul' he says to himself 'thou hast goods laid up for many years, even for ever. Although the Lord does not manifest Himself to you any more, be neither uneasy nor afraid; He changes not'. Sometimes the delusion grows to such an extent that the further this man goes from the Kingdom of God, the stronger he imagines his faith. He even speaks contemptuously of that Kingdom. He calls *righteousness, peace,* and *joy in the Holy Ghost* an immature experience, a low dispensation, beyond which he has now happily passed. He thanks God he can now rest upon the bare Word, without an application of it to his heart; that is to say, he is fully satisfied with the letter without the Spirit, he feeds upon the empty husks of notions and opinions, as if they were power and life.

The end of this dreadful mistake is generally a relapse into gross sin, as witness the falls of David and Solomon;

45

or, what is not much better, he settles into a form of godliness without the power of the same, like the Laodiceans of old. The only way to avoid this precipice, is for us to follow in the light of the first manifestation, and to look daily for new visitations from Christ, until He makes His abode with us, and until we walk in the light as He is in the light. A manifestation of the Holy Spirit last year will no more support a soul this year, than air breathed yesterday will nourish the flame of life today. The sun which warmed us last week, must shine again this week; old light is dead light; a notion of old warmth is a very cold notion; we must have fresh food daily, and though we need not a new Christ, we need—perpetually—new displays of His eternal love and power. The Lord taught us this important lesson when He made the manna in the wilderness to disappear every day, and when He caused that manna which was not gathered fresh, to breed worms and to stink.[1]

Nevertheless, even as the mysterious food continued sweet in the golden pot within the ark, so does the heavenly power in Christ; to whom, every true Israelite will come daily for new supplies of His hidden manna, for fresh manifestations of the Holy Spirit. Thousands, by not taking account of this, seek the living among the dead, fancying that a living Saviour is to be found in dead experiences, and that all is well even though they live after the flesh, and are, perhaps, even led captive by the devil, at his will. However, when their souls awake out of this dangerous dream, they will become aware of their mistake,

[1] The critic and the extremist may consider that Mr. Fletcher is here advocating weekly sights of the Saviour. Nothing is further from the truth, as the author is at pains to make clear. However, he does advocate constant close contact with the One who said 'without Me you can do nothing': Editor.

and will frankly acknowledge 'God is not the God of the dead, but of the living' and that 'if after they have escaped the pollutions of the world, through the knowledge of the Lord and Saviour Jesus Christ, they are again entangled therein, and overcome, the latter end is worse with them than the beginning.'

IV The Measure of Revelations

It is undeniable that some persons are blessed with clearer, stronger, or earlier manifestations than others; but why this is so, is one of the mysteries of God's Kingdom that shall not be explained until the day of judgment. In the meantime, the following reflections may possibly cast some light on the subject, and help you to affirm that the Lord does all things well.

1. Our Lord suits the manifestations of Himself to the various states of the Church. Under the Mosaic dispensation, which consisted much in externals, divine manifestations had—generally—some external circumstances. However, the Christian Church—being formed upon a more spiritual basis—is favoured with revelations of a more spiritual and internal nature.

2. The Lord considers us to be rational creatures, in a state of probation. Were he to indulge us with powerful, incessant, overwhelming revelations of Himself, He would be forcing us, rather than gently leading us, to repentance and obedience. Every day is not another day of Pentecost. Soon after the Son of God had seen the 'heavens open', He was *led* into the wilderness to be tried by the devil; and so is His spouse after Him. Paul, by his observation that he was 'not disobedient to the heavenly vision', and that he 'kept his body under, lest he should become a castaway', intimates that his bright manifestation was not of such continuance and force, and that he might have disobeyed as Jonah did in a similar situation. In fact, some

have resisted bright manifestations in their day; in this connection, consider Cain, Judas, Balaam, Saul, Nebuchadnezzar, and the Israelites who perished in the wilderness; and too many backsliders are resisting them now! Even as there is a time of trial for faith, hope, and patience, there is also an abatement of the power which attends divine manifestations.

3. Our wise Redeemer proportions the means to the end. If the effect of a manifestation of His love is to be exceedingly great, the manifestation must be exceedingly bright. Suppose the burden of guilt and hardness, temptation and sorrow, under which one groans, is ten times greater than that which oppresses another, it is plain that the manifestation which is to remove the tenfold weight is to be ten times stronger. The same rule holds also with regard to sufferings and labours. The hotter the fight of afflictions which God's children are to go through, the stronger and brighter also is the celestial armour put upon them at the revelation of the Captain of their Salvation.

4. Neither can it be doubted that our good Lord, in fixing the degree of divine manifestation, has a particular respect to the state and capacity of the souls to whom He reveals Himself. The deeper that sinners mourn for Him the deeper He makes them drink of the cup of salvation at His appearing. Blessed are they that greatly hunger and thirst after righteousness; their souls are thereby greatly enlarged to receive the oil of gladness, and the wine of the kingdom. Blessed are the poor in spirit, those whose souls are as empty as the vessels of the desolate widow in the time of Elisha; when the heavenly prophet shall visit them, the streams of His fullness shall certainly flow according to the degree of their emptiness.

5. A skilful physician prescribes weaker or stronger medicines, according to the state of his patients; so does the Physician of souls. He weighs, if I may so speak, every

dram of the heavenly power in the scales of goodness and wisdom. He knows what quantity of the heavenly cordial our spirits can bear, and will not—without the greatest care—put the strong wine of His powerful love into a weak vessel. He sees, that as some persons can stand—for a time—the sight of the noon-day sun, when others are hurt by the first appearance of a candle, so some Christians can bear the strong beams of His gracious presence, while others are almost overpowered by His fainter rays.

6. If some live and die without manifestations of the Redeemer's love and glory, the reasons of it may possibly be found in the depths of His justice and goodness. They *grieve*, and *quench* the Holy Spirit, who convinces the world of sin; and it is very fit they should not have him as a *Comforter*, whom they obstinately reject as a *Reprover*. Add to this, our Lord's ability to foresee how such people, if favoured with tokens of His more distinguishing condescension, would only abuse them (as Cain and the Pharisees did); knowing their intentions, He does not put them to the trial, nor allows them to add to their guilt by trampling mercy and love under foot. In other words, this seeming severity is, in fact, true kindness.

7. The Lord not only proportions the degree of His powerful appearance to the weakness of our souls, but also to that of our bodies. He knows what we are made of, and remembers that we are but flesh. If the natural sun (that glorious emblem of our Emmanuel) were to come close to our earth and shine as bright as possible, the insufferable blaze and heat would instantly blind and consume us. In simple comparison, if our bright Sun of Righteousness were to manifest His unclouded glory, or to appear without the tempering medium of His manhood, no flesh could support the sight. The brain, unable to bear the high operations of the soul, would snap; the heart of the

wicked, swelled with intolerable pangs of fear, and that of the righteous, dilated by overwhelming transports of joy, would instantly burst. God, therefore, is aware that no man can see His face, without some dimming veil, and live. It was with this in mind that Manoah and others, after the Lord had manifested Himself to them, showed anxiety for their human lives.

8. Perhaps this may help us to account for the reason why the Lord still hides His face from some of His sincere seekers. They sit begging by the wayside of His ordinances, and yet He does not pass by in such a manner that their spiritual sight is restored, in order that they might know Him. In all probability He designs for them a manifestation which is more bright than they are capable of bearing. When their hearts are strong enough for the heavenly vision, it will be granted to them; let them only wait for it. Let patience have her perfect work, and let faith in God's Word be tried to the uttermost; then, He that cometh, will come, and will not tarry; He will bring His reward with Him, and one moment of His presence will make them abundantly glad that they waited for an age. Were He to appear before they were prepared, by the humiliation of repentance and the patience of hope, they would be like those carnal Israelites, who—far from being able to commune with God—could not so much as speak to Moses (after he came down from the mount) without first obliging him to put a veil over his shining face.

APOSTOLIC REVELATIONS

Peter, James, and John, were—it seems—the foremost of the Apostles in spiritual strength and boldness; nevertheless, the manifestation which they had of Christ on the mount of transfiguration almost overwhelmed them. Their bodies sank under the weight of glory, and when they came

51

out of their sleep (or trance) they could not recover themselves; they knew not what they said. This had happened previously to Daniel, and later to John the beloved Apostle, who, when he saw his Saviour with some additional beams of glory, fell at His feet as though dead. Paul not only lost his sight on such an occasion, but was near to losing his life—being unable to take any refreshment for three days and three nights. It is also generally supposed that Moses actually died under the overpowering displays of the Redeemer's love. Hence, we learn that God's way and time are best, and that we are to leave both to His gracious wisdom; He using the means by which He has promised to manifest Himself to those who diligently seek Him.

MAN'S PART IN THIS

If you desire to know the Lord in a more intimate way, you will need to use what means are available to you. The agent or author of every divine manifestation is the eternal God, one in three and three in one. The Father reveals His Son, the Lord Jesus Christ shows Himself, and the Holy Spirit freely testifies of Him. Nevertheless, the Scriptures—in general—attribute the wonder of divine manifestations to the blessed Spirit. No man can, experimentally, say that Jesus is the Lord, but by the Holy Ghost. It is His peculiar office to convince the world of righteousness, by enabling us to know the Lord our Righteousness in a saving way. 'He shall glorify me' said Christ 'for He shall take of Mine, and shall shew it unto you'; and this He does, without any merit of ours, by the means which God has appointed, and which He enables us to use aright.

The means are both outward and inward; the outward are what the Church calls 'The Means of Grace' which are: particularly hearing or reading God's Word, partaking of the sacraments, and praying together with one accord for the manifestation of the Spirit as the early Christians did. These means are to be used with the greatest diligence, but not to be altogether trusted; the only proper object of our confidence is God Himself, who works all in all. It was not Moses' rod which parted the Red Sea, but that almighty arm which once divided water from water without a rod. Nevertheless, Moses could not throw his rod away, under the pretence of trusting in God alone, even as he could not rely on the mere instrument, as if divine power resided in it.

Though the Lord works by means, in general, He ties Himself to none of them, and sometimes works without any. The same Spirit which fell upon Cornelius while Peter preached, fell upon Peter on the day of Pentecost, without any preaching. And the same Lord who opened Lydia's heart by the ministry of Paul, opened the heart of Paul by the sole exertion of His own power. From this we learn that, whilst on the one hand we must not, like the profane and the extremists, tempt the Lord by neglecting the use of any of the means He has appointed, so on the other hand, we must beware of confining God to particular means, times, and places, in the way that the bigoted and superstitious do. Remember that when we are cut off from all outward means, it is our privilege to wait for the immediate display of God's arm, in the use of the *inward* means.

Concerning these inward means, the first is to believe that there will be a performance of the Lord's promise, and that He is both willing and able to manifest Himself to us, in a way that He does not do to the world; this is the very root of prayer, fervency, hope, and expectation! Without the action of this preparatory faith, the soul droops and becomes an easy prey to despondency, vanity, or sloth. Where this talent is buried, the Lord seldom works. 'Believest thou, that I am able to do this for you?' is generally the first question He puts to the seeker's heart. If it is answered in the negative, He can do no great miracle, because of this unbelief. Nevertheless, it must be acknowledged that Paul was blessed with a revelation of the Son of God, without any previous desire or expectation of it. In him and some others it could be said that 'I was found of them that sought Me not; I was manifested to them that asked not after me.' However, in general— where the gospel is preached—the Lord will be *inquired of* by the house of Israel to do this; and if He visits any with conviction, as He did Paul, it is only to make them pray as that Apostle did, until He manifests Himself by the Holy Ghost, in consolation and love.

The second inward means by which one may encourage the manifestation of Christ is *resignation* as to the particular *manner*, *time*, and *place* of it. Through *patience*, as well as faith and prayer, we inherit the promised blessing. Some, trusting in their carnal wisdom and intellect, mark out the way in which salvation must come to their hearts; but the Lord generally disappoints these proud seekers, for believers are not born 'of the will of the flesh, nor of the will of man, but of God.' The Jews *expected* the Messiah, and in this they were right; but they expected Him *in their own way*, and here they stumbled and fell. While they looked for a mighty conqueror who would come to make them great, they overlooked the lowly Prince of Peace, who came to make them good; and—finally—they crucified Him as a base imposter. This disposition is in us all by nature; hence Christ is commonly rejected in the Spirit *by Christians*, as He was in the flesh by the Jews. We would have Him come in order to give us an idle rest, but He appears with the intention of teaching us to deny ungodliness and to fight the good fight of faith; this we do not find palatable. Our nature wants us to step up into a throne at once, but Christ offers first to nail us to the tree and to crucify our flesh with its affections and lusts; from this, we shrink as from the grave. We expect to be carried at once to the top of Mount Tabor, to see unutterable glory; He leads us to Gethsemane to watch and to pray, or else to Calvary to suffer and to die with him; at this we recoil, and do not choose to know Him. Our impatience dictates that He shall instantaneously turn our midnight into noon-day; but instead of manifesting Himself quickly like the meridian sun, He may, perhaps, appear only as the morning star. This defeats us; we despise the day of small things and do not consider that so meagre an appearance is worthy of our notice and thanks.

If you, reader, ever seek a personal knowledge of Jesus, never stop seeking Him until you witness your sun going down no more. However, in the meantime, never slight the least ray of the heavenly light; the least of these may open into the broad day of eternity. Cease from your own false wisdom, and become as a little child, or you will not enter the kingdom of heaven, nor see the King in His beauty.

The third and last inward means that I would recommend, is a tender regard for the *reproofs of the Spirit*. This means a constant attention to the drawings of the Father, obedience to the calls these have to secret prayer, together with a fear of depending upon such duties and not solely upon the faithfulness of Jesus. Whoever follows these directions—according to the grace given to him—will, of course, cease from outward evil and do—as he can—the little good his hands find to do. This is a better way of waiting for the revelation of Christ, than to lie down in dejection and hopeless unbelief. All those who sullenly bury their own talent, and wilfully retain the accursed thing, complain in vain that their Lord makes long tarrying. They obstinately grieve His convincing

Spirit and then absurdly clamour (because He does not reward them for it) for the comforts of His heavenly presence. Let us not be so unreasonable. Let us strive to enter in at the strait gate, remembering that many shall seek to enter in, but shall not be able. However let us strive *lawfully*, not making for ourselves a righteousness of our own seeking by our manner of knocking and striving. The sun does not shine because we deserve it through drawing back our curtains, but because it is in its nature so to shine. Jesus visits us, not because of any merit in our prayers or striving, but for His own sake— because His truth and compassion fail not. Free grace opens the door of mercy, not to works and merit, but to want and misery. That you and I may knock and press in, with all other needy, penitent, believing sinners, is the earnest wish of a heart which prompts me to write as I have done.

V Old Testament Manifestations

In an earlier chapter I wrote that, in my opinion, the Lord has regularly manifested Himself to His people, in every age. You may have found this assertion somewhat difficult to accept. Not wishing to have you misunderstand me, or think my views extreme, I would now like to prove that *scripture* and *history* are on my side.

I shall then, in this chapter, appeal to the manifestations recorded in the Old Testament. You cannot expect that all of the revelations of any particular child of God (much less those of everyone) to be mentioned in so short a document as that of the Bible. Nevertheless, enough is said on this point to convince me that in every age God has favoured the sons of men with special displays of His presence.

Let us go back as far as Adam himself. As you would expect, the Lord conversed with him *before* the Fall, when He presented Adam with a partner and when He brought every beast of the field before him, to see what Adam would call them. However, the Lord also visited him *after* the Fall, not only to pronounce His sentence, but also to promise that He would become the woman's seed, and bruise the serpent's head. And was not this manifestation granted to Abel, when the Lord had respect to his sacrifice—the very cause of Cain's envy, wrath, and murder! Did not Enoch's walk with God imply a constant union and communion with Emmanuel? And how could this union have taken place, if the Lord had not first revealed

Himself to the Patriarch? Must not two persons meet and agree, before they can walk and converse together?

We read that Noah *found grace* in the eyes of the Lord, and—in consequence of it—was made acquainted with His righteous designs, and received directions how to escape from a perishing world. The story of Abraham is full of accounts of such manifestations. In one of them, the Lord called him out of his sins, and from his kindred, to go to both the heavenly and the earthly Canaan. In other revelations, he promised Abraham a son, Isaac, and Isaac's mysterious seed. Several years after, for the trial of his faith, God commanded him to sacrifice his son; and when the trial was over, He declared His approval of Abraham's conduct. He even went further! Read Genesis 18 and see how the divine philanthropy appeared, in His condescending manner. to clothe Himself with the nature He was later to assume in the virgin's womb, and to converse—in this undress—with the father of the faithful, like a prince with his favourite, or as a friend with his confidant.

Sarah, Agar, Isaac, and Rebekah, all had their divine manifestations, but those of Jacob deserve our particular attention. When he fled to Syria, from the face of his brother Esau, and lay desolate in a field, having only a heap of stones for his pillow, the God of all consolation appeared to him and stood above a mysterious ladder, on which the angels of God ascended and descended, and said to him 'I am the Lord God of Abraham, thy father and the God of Isaac: the land whereon thou liest, to thee will I give it, and to thy seed . . . and, behold, I am with thee, and will keep thee in all places whither thou goest.

Jacob called that place Bethel, the house of God, and 'the gate of heaven'. This seems to have been an intimation that no one ever found the gate of heaven by his own efforts, but by a manifestation of Christ, who is alone the Way to the Father, and the door into glory. When th

58

same patriarch returned to Canaan, and was left alone one night, a Man wrestled with him until daybreak. Then, when this extraordinary person said 'Let me go, for the day breaketh' he replied 'I will not let thee go, except thou bless me'; and we read that 'he blessed him there', acknowledging that Jacob had *power with God*, even with Him whose name is Emmanuel. Jacob called the name of the place Peniel, for, he said 'I have seen God face to face, and my life is preserved. . . .' The design of this manifestation was merely to strengthen Jacob's faith, and we learn from it that the children of faithful Abraham may wrestle in prayer with the Lord, as Jacob did, until they prevail and are blessed in the way that he was.

Moses was favoured with numerous manifestations, sometimes because of his official position as a leader, and at other times only on the grounds of him being a common believer. 'And the Angel of the Lord[1] appeared unto him, in a flame of fire out of the midst of a bush; and he looked, and behold, the bush burned with fire, and the bush was not consumed . . . And when the Lord saw that he turned aside to see the bush, God called unto Moses out of the midst of the bush.' Many witnessed a sight which was equally glorious, however, on another occasion: 'Moses, Aaron, Nadab, Abihu and seventy of the elders of Israel saw the God of Israel; there was under His feet as it were a paved work of sapphire stone, and as it were the body of heaven in its clearness. And upon the nobles of the children of Israel He laid not His hand; also they saw God, and did eat and drink.' Sometimes all Israel shared in the manifestation: 'They all drank of that spiritual

[1] The reader may be surprised to see that the author is equating this special angel with the Son of God. If he refers to the opinions of our forefathers he will discover that this is not an unusual idea. In fact, the 1967 Inter-Varsity Fellowship commentary on Genesis says as much: Editor.

Rock that followed them' comments Paul 'and that rock was Christ.' The cloud of the Lord was upon the tabernacle by day, according to the Jewish historian, and fire was upon it by night, in the sight of *all* the house of Israel. 'It came to pass, as Moses entered into the tabernacle, the cloudy pillar descended, and stood at the door of the tabernacle, and the Lord talked with Moses. And *all* the people saw the cloudy pillar ... *all* the people rose up and worshipped, every man in his tent door. And the Lord spake unto Moses face to face, as a man speaketh unto his friend.'

So gracious was Emmanuel to Moses, that when this Jewish leader said 'I beseech thee, shew me thy glory' the Lord answered 'I will make all My goodness pass before thee ... but thou canst not see My face, for there shall no man see Me and live.' These displays of divine goodness and glory left a deep impression upon even the countenance of the man of God; his face shone in such a glorious way that the children of Israel were afraid to come near him, and he was obliged to put a veil over his face before conversing with them. Though this appears to be very extraordinary, the Apostles inform us that the change which took place in the countenance of Moses, now occurs in the souls of believers. By faith they behold the Lord through the glass of gospel promises and, beholding Him, they are made 'partakers of the divine nature'—changed into the same image from glory to glory.

Joshua, Moses' successor, was blessed with many similar manifestations, each of which conveyed to him new degrees of courage and wisdom. To give one example only: when Joshua was by Jericho, he lifted up his eyes and looked, and behold, there stood a man over against him, with his sword drawn in his hand; and Joshua went up to him, and said to him 'Art thou for us, or for our adversaries?' And he said 'Nay, but as Captain of the host of the Lord am I now come'. And Joshua (aware that it was Jehovah speaking) fell on his face to the earth, worshipped his Visitor, and said 'What saith my Lord unto His servant?' And the Captain of the Lord's host said to Joshua 'Loose thy shoe from off thy foot; for the place whereon thou standest is holy'; and Joshua did so. Every true personal discovery of Christ has a similar effect; it humbles us and makes us worship Him. Those who are blessed by an open revelation see *holiness to the Lord* written upon every surrounding object; they are loosed from earth and earthly things, and the towering walls of sin fall down, like those of Jericho fell down soon after this manifestation occurred to Joshua.

After Joshua's death a heavenly person, called the Angel of the Lord, came from Gilgal to Bochim and spake such words to all the children of Israel, that the people were universally melted; 'they lifted up their voice and wept . . . and they sacrificed there unto the Lord.' Nothing can so effectually make sinners relent as a sight of Him whom they have pierced; when they have such a revelation, whatever place they are in becomes a Bochim, a valley of tears and adoration.

Not long after this, the Lord manifested Himself to Deborah; by the wisdom and fortitude communicated to her in that revelation, she was enabled to judge Israel and lead desponding Barak to certain victory, through 900 chariots of iron.

The condescension of our Emmanuel appears in a still more striking light in the manifestation which He granted to Gideon. The mysterious Angel of the Lord (repeatedly called Jehovah) came and sat under an oak in Ophrah, and after appearing to Gideon, said 'The Lord is with thee . . . and thou shalt smite the Midianites as one man.' And the Lord looked upon him (what a courage-inspiring look this was: as powerful, no doubt, as that which met cursing Peter's eye and brought repentance to his heart!) and said, 'Go in this thy might ... have not I sent thee?' And Gideon said 'Alas, O Lord God! for because I have seen an Angel of the Lord face to face.' And the Lord said unto him 'Peace be unto thee; fear not; thou shalt not die.' Thus strengthened and comforted, Gideon built an altar to Jehovah-Shalom and threw down the altar of Baal. From this, we learn that when Jesus manifests Himself to a sinner. He fills him with a noble contempt of the devil and gives him an effectual resolution to break down Satan's altars, together with a divine courage to shake off the yoke of the spiritual Midianites. He imparts to an awakened sinner a comfortable assurance that the bitterness of death is past, and that *Jehovah Shalom*, the God of peace, even *Christ our peace*, is with him; and the sinner, constrained by the love of Christ, offers his believing heart and makes sacrifices of thanksgiving on that best of altars. In this way, there begins a free exchange between the Lord and a modern Gideon—only of a far more spiritual and more delightful nature.

Some years later, the same Angel of God appeared to Manoah's wife, and promised her a son. Her husband prayed for the same manifestation and God hearkened to his voice; the heavenly Personage manifested Himself a second time. Manoah asked Him for His name, and the Angel said to him 'Why askest thou thus after My name, seeing it is secret?' Manoah offered a burnt offering; the Angel received it at his hands and, while He ascended in the flame of the altar, Manoah fell on his face to the ground; he knew that this was the Angel Jehovah and so he said to his wife 'We shall surely die, because we have seen God.' However, in due course, the birth of Samson (and not their death) resulted from this unusual two-fold manifestation.

There was a time when Samuel did not *know* the Lord,

and also when the Word of the Lord (that Word which was afterwards made flesh) was not *revealed* to him. The devoted youth worshipped 'in the dark' until the Lord *appeared again* in Shiloh, until He *came, stood,* and *called* Samuel. From that memorable time, the Lord was *with* him, and he did not let any of God's words 'fall to the ground'. The fellowship between God and this prophet soon grew to such a degree that the sacred historian says *the Lord told him in his ear* what He wanted Samuel to know.

David had many manifestations of Christ, and of His pardoning love; and, far from supposing this blessing peculiar to himself (as a prophet) he declared that '*for this shall every one that is godly pray unto Thee Lord, when thou mayest be found.*' He knew his Shepherd's inward voice so well that, without it, no outward message (though ever so comfortable) could restore peace to his troubled mind. When he had been convinced of his sins of adultery and murder (by the close application of Nathan's parable) the prophet assured David that the Lord had *put away his sin* and so *he should not die.* Such a report would content many of our modern penitents, but nothing short of a full and ready manifestation of our forgiving God could comfort the royal mourner—'Wash thou me' he prayed 'and I shall be clean'. Nathan's words of comforting assurance, though ever so true in their way, could not give David an awareness of forgiveness; 'speak thyself merciful Lord and make me to hear joy and gladness, so that the bones which thou hast broken may rejoice.'

Solomon was favoured with a quite remarkable revelation: In Gibeon, to which place Solomon had gone to sacrifice, the Lord appeared unto him in a dream by night; and God said 'Ask what I shall give thee'. And Solomon said ... 'Give, therefore, thy servant an understanding heart' ... The speech pleased the Lord ... and

God said unto him 'Because thou hast asked this thing . . . I have done according to thy words: lo, I have given thee a wise and understanding heart . . . and that which thou hast not asked, both riches and honour.' Though this promise was made to Solomon in a dream only, he knew by the change which he found in himself, after he awoke, and by the powerful evidence which accompanies divine manifestations, that it was glorious reality. Fully persuaded of the promise, he did not hesitate to offer peace-offerings and to make a feast for all of his servants, to mark the occasion. Nor was this the only time Solomon was thus favoured: when he had finished building the temple and had prayed for a blessing upon it, the Lord appeared to him *a second time*, as He had appeared to him in Gibeon and said 'I have heard thy prayer'.

Elijah has always been famous for the power which he had, through the prayer of faith, to obtain divine manifestations, that James—in his Epistle—uses him as an example to the church, for a pattern of successful 'wrestling with God'. Who is the God of Elijah but that same Lord Who manifests Himself to His worshippers still, in opposition to Baal and other false gods! The Lord answered Elijah by fire at the foot of Mount Carmel, and by showers on the top of the same. When Elijah lodged in Mount Horeb, in a cave 'Behold, the Word of the Lord came to him . . . "What dost thou here, Elijah?" . . . "Go forth and stand upon the mount before the Lord". And behold, the Lord passed by.'

Micaiah, another man of God 'saw the Lord sitting on His throne, and all the host of heaven standing by Him on His right hand and on His left.'

Elisha was not only blessed with frequent manifestations of the Lord and of His power, but also of His heavenly retinue. He saw in an hour of danger 'the mountain full of horses and chariots of fire' ready to protect him. And, at his request, the Lord condescended to open Elisha's servant's eyes, so that his drooping spirit might be revived.

Job, after long debates with his friends, met with the Lord Himself 'out of a whirlwind' and saw a manifestation which caused him to utter these famous words: 'I have heard of Thee by the hearing of the ear, but now mine eye seeth Thee. Wherefore I abhor myself, and repent in dust and ashes.' From this, we learn that nothing apart from a personal discovery of the Lord can silence vain reasonings and unbelieving fears; a revelation of the Lord, alone, makes us to lie prostrate at our Maker's feet.

John, in his Gospel, informs us that Isaiah *saw* Christ's glory and spoke of Him, when he described the glorious manifestation in which he received a new seal of pardoning and sanctifying love: 'I saw the Lord sitting upon a throne, high and lifted up, and His train filled the temple' ... 'then said I "Woe is me! for I am undone; because I am a man of unclean lips, and I dwell in the midst of a people of unclean lips; for mine eyes have seen the King, the Lord of Hosts". Then flew one of the seraphims unto me, having a live coal in his hand ... from off the altar ... he said ... "Thine iniquity is taken away, and thy sin purged" ...' Many are not truly aware of the forgiveness of their sins, until they see—by faith—the Lord of Hosts, and are melted into repentance, then inflamed with love at the glorious sight. Isaiah not only beheld Christ's glory, but was blessed with the clearest view of His sufferings. He saw Him as 'a man of sorrows, acquainted with grief.' These revelations were not only intended for the good of the Church later, but also for the establishment of the prophet's faith then.

I shall not mention those of Ezekiel, for they are so numerous that a complete account of them would fill a book alone. I suggest that you re-read the Second Book of Kings, with this subject in mind, in order to recall the wonder of those days.

Jeremiah, speaking of God's people, wrote that the Lord had appeared to him, saying 'Yea, I have loved thee with an everlasting love; therefore with loving kindness have I drawn thee.' Daniel enjoyed the same favour: 'I beheld ... the Ancient of Days ... and one like the Son of Man came with the clouds of heaven.' We may assume that Daniel's three hebrew companions, Shadrach, Meshach, and Abed-nego, were also aware of their heavenly Deliverer's presence. In fact, they must have been more concerned at the discovery than Nebuchadnezzar, who himself cried out 'Lo, I see four men loose, walking in the midst of the fire, and they have no hurt; and the form of the fourth is like the Son of God.'

It would be absurd to suppose that the lesser prophets, and other men of God down through the centuries, to whom the word of the Lord came, had no awareness of the Lord himself—the essential Word. If some display of His presence had not attended their every revelation, might they not have said 'Thus saith my warm imagination'; 'Thus saith my enthusiastic brain', instead of 'Thus saith the Lord'?

From the variety and authenticity of these manifestations left upon sacred record, I conclude that the doctrine which I maintain—far from being new and unscriptural— is supported by the experiences of God's children from the creation of the world until the close of the Old Testament.

Concerning what is *extraordinary* (as to the design and circumstances of some of these manifestations) I refer you to the distinction which I made on that subject in the third chapter. Should you raise the objection that the contents of that chapter prove only that God favoured the Patriarchs and Jews with immediate revelations of Himself, *because they had neither the Gospel nor the Scriptures*, I answer:

1. The Gospel was preached *to them*, as well as to us. The Patriarchs had tradition, which answered the end of the Scriptures in their day; the Jews, in the time of the Judges, had not only tradition but a considerable part of the Scriptures also, consisting of—at least—all the writings of Moses. Under the kings they had the Psalms, Job, Ecclesiastes, the Proverbs, and a thousand and five songs of Solomon, only one of which has been handed down to our times. They had also the book of Nathan the prophet, the prophecy of Ahijah the Shilonite, and the visions of Iddo the seer, which are now lost. These contained the substance of the Bible.

2. When the Lord answered Saul no more—neither by prophets nor by dreams—the reason assigned for it by the Holy Spirit is not that the canon of Scripture was filled (so that there was no further need for open revelations), but that the Lord *was departed from him*, and *had become his enemy*!

3. David (who had the honour of being a sacred writer himself), after his relapse into sin, could no longer find satisfaction in the Psalms he had written, but mourned, prayed, and watered his bed with his tears; he could not be calmed until the Lord revealed His pardoning love to him, saying to his soul 'I am thy salvation'.

4. If, because we have the letter of Scripture, we must be deprived of all immediate manifestations of Christ and of his Spirit, we are great losers by that blessed Book, and we might reasonably say 'Lord, bring us back to the dispensation of Moses. Thy Jewish servants could formerly converse with Thee face to face, but now we can know

nothing of Thee except by their writings. They viewed Thy glory in various wonderful appearances, but we are left only with black lines telling us of Thy glory. They had the bright Shekinah; we have only obscure descriptions of it. They were blessed with lively oracles; we only with dead letters. The ark of Thy covenant went before them, and struck terror into all their adversaries, but a book of which our enemies make daily sport, is the only revelation of Thy power among us. They made their boast of Urim and Thummin, and received immediate answers from between the Cherubim; but we have only general ones, by means of Hebrew and Greek writings, which many do not understand. They conversed familiarly with Moses their mediator, with Aaron their high-priest, and with Samuel their prophet; these holy men gave them unerring directions in doubtful cases; but alas! . . . the Apostles and inspired men are all dead, and Thou, Lord Jesus, our Mediator, Priest, and Prophet, may not be consulted to any purpose, for Thou dost manifest Thyself no more! As for Thy sacred Book, Thou knowest that sometimes the want of money to purchase it, the want of learning to consult the original, the want of wisdom to understand translations, the want of skill or sight to read it, prevent our making the most of it, and keep some from reaping any benefit from it at all. O Lord, if because we have this blessed picture of Thee, we must have no discovery of the glorious Original, have compassion on us, take back Thy precious book, and impart Thy more precious Self to us, as Thou didst do to Thine ancient people.'

5. Paul declared, that although the Mosaic dispensation was *glorious*, that of Christ *exceeds it* in glory! However, if Christ revealed Himself to the Jews, but to Christians only by the letter of a Book, it is plain that the Apostle was mistaken. How can anyone deny that it is far more

glorious to see the light of God's countenance and to hear His voice, than merely to read something about them?

6. Particular manifestations of Christ, far from ceasing with the Jewish era *have increased in brightness and spirituality* during the Christian dispensation. I shall endeavour to prove this to you in the next chapter.

VI New Testament Manifestations

As promised, I now hope to prove that the New Testament also abounds with accounts of special revelations of the Son of God.

Before His birth, Jesus manifested Himself to the Virgin Mary by the overshadowing power of the Holy Spirit. She rejoiced *in God her Saviour* and was more thankful that He had revealed Himself as God in her soul, than she was to find Him conceived as Man in her womb. Soon after, Joseph was assured in a heavenly dream, that the child Mary had conceived was *Emmanuel* 'God with us'. The Lord revealed Himself next to Elizabeth: when she heard the salutation of Mary, she was *filled with the Holy Ghost*, and made aware of the fact that Mary, though a virgin, was the mother of her Lord. So powerful was this manifestation that her own unborn son John was affected by it—'The babe leaped in her womb' ... and was filled with the Holy Ghost *even from his mother's womb*!

So important is a personal knowledge of Jesus that an angel directed the shepherds, and a miraculous star the wise men, to the place where He was born and was living. And the Holy Ghost did so reveal Him to their hearts that they did not hesitate to worship the apparently insignificant infant, as the majestic God of heaven and earth!

Simeon, who waited 'for the consolation of Israel', had it 'revealed unto him, by the Holy Ghost', that he should not see death, before he had seen the Lord's Christ. The promise was fulfilled; whilst his bodily eyes saw nothing but a poor infant, presented without pomp in the temple, Simeon's spiritual eyes perceived Him to be the Light of Israel, and the Salvation of God. Nor was this extraordinary favour granted only to Simeon, for it is written that 'all flesh shall see the salvation of God' and it is Luke who informs us that Anna shared this sight with the old Israelite, giving thanks to her new-born Lord, speaking of him 'to all that looked for redemption' in Jerusalem.

When Jesus entered upon His ministry, He first manifested Himself to his forerunner, John the Baptist. 'I knew Him not' said John 'but He that sent me to baptize with water, the same said unto me "Upon whom thou shalt see the Spirit descending, and remaining on Him, the same is He who baptizes with the Holy Ghost". And I saw, and bear record that this is the Son of God.'

Jesus manifested Himself, in a spiritual way, to Nathaniel under a fig tree, and the honest Israelite—being reminded of that divine favour—confessed the author of it: 'Rabbi' he said 'thou art the Son of God, thou art the King of Israel.' Our Lord, pleased with this ready confession, promised that He should see greater things and enjoy brighter manifestations than this; that he should even 'see the heavens open, and the angels of God ascending and descending upon the Son of man.'

The plain outward appearance of our Saviour, together with His miracles, tended rather to confound (instead of convert) the beholders. What glorious beams of His Godhead must have pierced through the veil of His mean appearance, when—with supreme authority—He turned the money changers out of the temple; when He entered Jerusalem in triumph, and all the city was moved; and when He said to those who apprehended him in Gethsemane 'I am He' and they fell on the ground! Nevertheless, we do not learn of anyone being blessed with a saving knowledge of Him on any of these wonderful occasions. The people of Galilee saw most of Him and yet believed least in Him. 'Whence hath this man wisdom, and these mighty works' they said, being astonished. In fact, 'they were offended at him'. Some went so far as to ascribe His miracles to a diabolical power, affirming that He cast out devils by Beelzebub, the prince of devils. So, it appears that if He had not—in some degree—revealed Himself inwardly to the hearts of the disciples, they would not have been ready to forsake all and follow Him immediately. He 'manifested forth his glory' writes John, concerning the Cana miracle 'and His disciples believed on Him', and yet when the manifestation was purely external, how weak was the effect it produced even upon them? Was not our Lord, after all, obliged to upbraid them with their *unbelief*, their *little faith*, and on one particular occasion, with their having *no faith*! If we know, in a saving way, that Jesus is 'God with us', *flesh and blood*, mere man—with all his best powers—has not revealed this to us; it has come from our Father who is in heaven. Even as 'no man knoweth the Father save the Son, and He to whom the Son will reveal Him', so no man knoweth the Son but the Father, and those to whom the Spirit (proceeding from the Father) does reveal Him. 'For no man can (in a saving way) say, that Jesus is the Lord, but by the Holy Ghost.' Also, 'He that hath seen me' (by this divine revelation) said Jesus 'hath seen the Father also; for I and the Father are one.'

If our Lord had not revealed Himself in a special manner to sinners, no one would have suspected Him to be 'God manifest in the flesh'. Until he shows Himself to us, in a way that He does not do to the unbelieving world, 'He hath no form nor comeliness; and when we see Him there is no beauty that we should desire Him; we hide as it were our faces from Him; He is despised, and we esteem Him not.' Our Lord was obliged to say to the woman of Samaria 'I that speak unto thee am He' and to say it with power so that it penetrated her heart, before she could believe with her heart unto righteousness. Only then, having been divinely wrought upon, did she run to inform her neighbours, so that they might draw living water out of the well of salvation which she had so happily found.

If our Lord had not called Zaccheus inwardly, as well as outwardly; if He had not made him come down from the pinnacle of proud nature, as well as from the sycamore tree; if He had not honoured the man's heart with His spiritual presence, just as He did his house with His bodily presence, would the rich publican have received Him gladly? And if not, would the Lord have said 'This day is salvation come to this house, forasmuch as Zaccheus is also a son of Abraham'?

Salvation did not enter into the heart of Simon the Pharisee, who admitted our Lord to his house and table, in the way that He came to Zaccheus. The penitent woman, who kissed His feet and washed them with her tears, obtained a blessing which the self-righteous Pharisee despised. It was to her contrite spirit, and not to his callous heart, that the Lord revealed Himself, as a pardoning God.

The blind man, restored to his bodily sight, did not know his heavenly Benefactor, until a second (and greater) miracle was wrought upon the eyes of his blind understanding. You will recall that Jesus found him, some time after he was cured, and said to him 'Dost thou believe on the Son of God?' The healed man answered 'Who is he, Lord, that I might believe on him?' And Jesus, opening the eyes of his mind, and manifesting Himself to this person, as He does not do to everyone, said 'Thou hast both seen Him, and it is He that talketh with thee'. Then, but not until then, could he say from his heart 'Lord I believe'.

Both of the thieves, who were crucified with Jesus, heard His prayers and strong cries; both saw His patience and His meekness, His wounds and His blood; one of them made sport of His sufferings, as though he had been the worst malefactor of the three; the other thief, blessed with an internal revelation of Christ's Person, implored His mercy, trusted Him with his soul, and confessed Him to be the King of glory, at the very moment when Jesus was dying like a base slave.

Peter wrote so highly of the manifestation with which he and two other disciples were favoured on the mount of transfiguration, that we ought not to omit a reference to it here. They saw the kingdom of God coming with power; they beheld the King in His beauty; 'we were eyewitnesses of His majesty, for He received from God the Father honour and glory, when there came such a voice to Him from the excellent glory "This is my beloved Son, in whom I am well pleased". And this voice which came from heaven, we heard.'

AFTER THE RESURRECTION

Nor did our Lord reveal Himself less, after His resurrection. You will remember that Mary sought Him at the grave with tears, and, as she turned around, she saw Him standing there, but *did not know* that it was Jesus. He said to her 'Why weepest thou? Whom seekest thou?' She, supposing him to be the gardener, inquired after the Object of her love. It was not until Jesus, after calling her by her name, manifested Himself to her as alive from the

74

dead, that she realised that here was her Master. Then, in rapture, she sought to take her old place at His feet, but was restrained.

With equal condescension Jesus appeared to Simon Peter, so that he might not be swallowed up by too much sorrow. True mourners of the Christian faith weep, some for an absent God—as Mary, others for their sins—as Peter, but they cannot be comforted—even by angels; they can only find true joy in Him who is nigh to all that call upon Him, and is health to those who are broken in heart. That One who appeared first to weeping Mary, and next to sorrowing Peter, will shortly visit spiritual mourners with His salvation. He is already *with them*, as he was with Mary, even though they do not realise it; He will soon be *in them*, the sure and comfortable hope of glory.

This observation is further confirmed by the experience of those two disciples who walked to Emmaus, immediately after the Resurrection, and were sad. Jesus drew near, joined, and comforted them; He made their hearts to burn within them as He talked with them along the road, and opened to them the Scriptures. But even so, their eyes were not *opened* so that they recognised Him; indeed, it was not until He sat down to eat with them 'that their eyes were opened and they knew him' in the breaking of bread. Unfortunately, many professors of religion in these days *are* satisfied with what *did not* satisfy the two disciples. They understood the Scriptures, their hearts burned with love and joy, Jesus was with them; but they knew Him not, until the happy moment when He fully opened the eye of their faith, and poured the light of His countenance on their ravished spirits. Happy are those who, like them, constrain an unknown Jesus—by mighty prayers—to tarry with them, until the veil is taken away from their hearts, and until they 'know in whom they have believed'.

The manifestations of Jesus to his disciples, as you will

know, were frequent between His Resurrection and His Ascension. An angel appeared to two of the holy mourners and said to them 'Fear not; for I know that ye seek Jesus, who was crucified. He is not here; for He is risen.' As they ran with fear and great joy to tell the rest of the disciples, Jesus met them and they held Him by His feet, and worshipped Him. The same day in the evening, when the doors were bolted for fear of the Jews, Jesus came and stood in the midst; they were terrified; He said 'Peace be unto you'. Then He shewed them His hands and His feet, ate with them as He had done of old with Abraham, and —to testify an inward manifestation of the Holy Ghost— He breathed upon them (as the Holy Spirit might breathe upon their minds) and thus He enabled them to understand the Scriptures. Out of condescension to Thomas, He shewed Himself to them a second time in a similar way; a third time at the sea of Tiberias; and 'after that He was seen of above five hundred brethren at once.'

AFTER THE ASCENSION

You may have held the opinion that these manifestations ceased when Christ had ascended up to heaven. I consider that this is true as far as manifestations of flesh and blood (or those that may be touched with material hands) are concerned. In other words, believers 'know Christ after the flesh no more'. Our Lord, by his gentle reproof to Thomas, *discountenanced our looking for carnal manifestations* of His person, and I have declared repeatedly that they are *not* what I contend for.

However, I must deny that *spiritual manifestations* of Christ ceased at His Ascension, if I am to continue to believe the Scriptures. Rather than ceasing, they became more frequent! For example, three thousand were 'pricked to the heart' on the day of Pentecost, and felt the need of a visit from the heavenly Physician. He then came to them, revealed in the power of his Spirit, with whom He is one. They received the gift of the Holy Ghost, whose office it is to manifest the Son. For 'the promise' was unto them 'and to your children, and to all that are afar off, even as many as the Lord our God shall call.' It was already true, as it has continued to be, that 'I am with you always, even unto the end of the world.'

Time would fail me to recount the stories of the five thousand who were converted some days later, of Cornelius and his household, and of Lydia and her household; in a word, of all who were truly brought to Christ in the early days of Christianity. The Lord 'opened their hearts; the Holy Ghost fell upon them; and they walked in His comforts.' Christ was evidently set forth crucified before their spiritual eyes; He dwelt in their hearts by faith; it was not they who lived, but Christ lived in them. They agreed with Paul that 'If any man have not the Spirit of Christ' (by whom He is savingly known) 'he is none of His.'

Stephen's experience is surely sufficient to decide the point. When brought before the council, they all *saw his face*, looking as if it was *the face of an angel*. Though *full of* the Holy Ghost, he wrought no miracle, he spoke no new tongue, but 'looked up steadfastly into heaven, and saw the glory of God, and Jesus standing on the right hand of God.' This manifestation was intended only for the private encouragement and comfort of the saintly deacon. However, his response to this revelation enraged the Jews more, and made them consider him to be a greater blasphemer, and a wilder enthusiast, than they had done before. So, stopping their ears, they ran upon him, cast him out of the city, and stoned him. Stephen, under the powerful influence of the private manifestation, kneeled down, called upon God in prayer, and said 'Lord Jesus receive my spirit. Lay not this sin to their charge.'

It is obvious, therefore, that nothing appears to be so absurd, to pharisees and formalists, as the doctrine which I here maintain. They lose all patience, when they are told that Christ has manifested Himself to one of His servants. No blasphemy can be compared with this, in the opinion of those who consider themselves to be wise, learned, and prudent. Also, it is obvious that the most exalted saints need fresh manifestations of the glory, love, and presence of Christ, if they are to depart this life with triumphant faith.

FOR ALL BELIEVERS

If you object that Stephen was specially favoured with this revelation because he was about to suffer for Christ, and that it would be a great presumption to expect similar support for all Christians, I reply with the five following observations:

1. We are called to suffer for Christ, as well as Stephen, although perhaps not in the same manner, or to the same degree.

2. We often need as much support from Christ as Stephen received, to stand against those children of men who are set on fire, whose teeth are spears and arrows, and whose tongues are a sharp sword; we need to quench the fiery darts of the devil, just as much as the martyr needed strength to stand against a shower of stones.

3. It is surely as hard to be racked with pain for years, or to burn several days in a fever, as you or I may be forced to do, as to be in a burning furnace for a few minutes, or to feel for a fleeting moment the anguish of a fractured skull, with our triumphant martyr.[1] No one

[1] Mr. Fletcher is not saying here that there is any genuine comparison between illness and martyrdom, but that believers have an intimate need of Christ when any form of suffering is inflicted upon them: Editor.

78

knows what pangs of body and agonies of soul may accompany the believer through the valley of the shadow of death. If our Lord Himself was not above being strengthened by an angel which came to Him from heaven, surely it is not fanatical to say that feeble creatures like ourselves may stand in need of a divine manifestation, in order to enable us to fight our last battle triumphantly.

4. We betray unbelief, if we suppose that Christ cannot do for us what He did for Stephen; and we betray our presumption if we say that we do not want any assistance.

5. The language of the Church of England makes her position clear: 'Grant' (says the Collect for St. Stephen's day) 'O Lord, that in all our sufferings here upon earth, for the testimony of thy truth, we may steadfastly look up to heaven, and—by faith—behold the glory that shall be revealed; and, being filled with the Holy Ghost, may learn to love and bless our persecutors, by the example of thy first martyr Saint Stephen, who prayed for his murderers to thee, O blessed Jesus, who standest at the right hand of God to succour all those who suffer for thee, our only Mediator and Advocate.'

You see, I have the suffrage of the Church! And, I believe that I have yours too, if you do not renounce all that Christendom stands for! Can you not see that if I am to be called an enthusiast for expecting myself to be filled with the Holy Spirit, and (by faith) to behold the glory that shall be revealed, just like Stephen, I am (at least) countenanced by a multitude of the finest men who have ever lived!

But, even if you reject the testimony of Stephen, and of all the clergy who testify to the reality and to the necessity of manifestations of our Lord, after His Ascension into heaven, I think that you, at least, accept that of Luke and Paul. They both inform us that whilst Saul of Tarsus was on his way to Damascus, the Lord—even Jesus—

appeared to him: Suddenly, there shone round about him a light from heaven (above the brightness of the sun) and he fell to the earth, and heard a voice saying unto him 'Saul, Saul, why persecutest thou Me? And he said 'Who art Thou, Lord?' And the Lord said 'I am Jesus, whom thou persecutest'. So powerful was the effect of this manifestation of Christ, that the infuriated sinner was converted immediately, and a fierce, blaspheming persecutor became a weeping, praying Apostle.

Do I hear you say 'True! Paul became an Apostle; but are all called to be Apostles?' No, we are not, but Christians are called to be converted from sin to holiness, and from the kingdom of darkness to the kingdom of God's dear Son! Paul's call to the Apostleship cannot be compared to his being made a child of God..Is it not true that Judas was a Christian by profession, an Apostle by his calling, and a devil by nature? And what is Judas compared to the meanest of God's children, or to poor Lazarus in Abraham's bosom? All who go to heaven are first 'turned from darkness to light, and from the power of Satan unto God'; this turning begins sometimes by a manifestation of Christ. In fact, I dare advance (upon the authority of one greater than Luke) that no conversion ever was completed without the revelation of the Son of God to the heart. 'I am the Way' said Jesus 'no man cometh to the Father, but *by Me*.' So, whilst it is true that we must 'look unto Christ' in order to be saved, our looking to Him for salvation will be to little purpose if Christ does not manifest Himself to us; it would be just as hopeless as our looking towards the East for rays of light, if it were true that the sun does not rise.[1]

[1] Some readers will not grasp this point easily, and some may be confused by the illustration. The author had met countless 'converts' who claimed that they had passed through an experience of 'looking to Christ' but who knew that they were no

The revelation of Christ which resulted in Saul's conversion was not the only one with which the Apostle was favoured. At Corinth, the Lord spoke to him by a vision, in the night: 'Be not afraid, but speak and hold not thy peace, for I am with thee, and no man shall set on thee to hurt thee.' On another occasion, apparently in order to wean him more from earth, Christ favoured him with intimate views of heaven. 'I knew a man in Christ' he wrote 'whether in the body I cannot tell, who was caught up to the third heaven, and heard unspeakable words, which it is not lawful for a man to utter.' Then, he informs us that 'lest I should be exalted above measure through the abundance of the revelations, there was given to me a thorn in the flesh, the messenger of Satan to buffet me.' After he had been brought before the Sanhedrin for preaching the Gospel, we are informed that the following night the Lord stood by him, and said 'Be of good cheer, Paul, for as thou hast testified of Me in Jerusalem, so must thou bear witness also at Rome.' Then, the ship in which he sailed was endangered by a storm, and 'the angel of God' stood by him and declared 'Fear not Paul'.

However, Paul was not the only one to whom Christ manifested Himself in this manner. Ananias of Damascus was not an Apostle (or even a deacon!) and yet the Lord spoke to him in a vision. After Ananias had replied, like Samuel, 'Behold, I am here, Lord' our Saviour said 'Arise, and go into the street which is called Straight, and enquire in the house of Judas for one called Saul of Tarsus; for behold he prayeth.' In a similar way, Philip was directed to go near, and join himself, to the Eunuch's chariot; and Peter being informed that three men were looking for him, heard the Holy Spirit say 'Arise, therefore, and get

different. Mr. Fletcher was unhappy about preaching which left people thinking that they need only 'look to Christ' and which did not encourage experimental religion: Editor.

thee down, and go with them, doubting nothing, for I have sent them.'

Whether we place these manifestations in the class of the extraordinary ones or of the mixed ones, we can learn these things from them: First, that the Lord Jesus Christ revealed Himself *as much* after His Ascension, as He did before. Secondly, that if He does this in order to send His servants with a gospel message to particular persons, He will do it much more in order to make that message effectual, and to bring salvation to those who wait for Him.

REVELATIONS IN REVELATION

As for the revelations which Christ made of Himself to John, there were so many that the last book of the New Testament is called *Revelation* and chiefly contains an account of them. 'I was in the Spirit on the Lord's day' we read of this Apostle, and he heard behind him a great voice, as of a trumpet, saying 'I am Alpha and Omega, the first and the last'. He turned to see who had spoken to him; and, having turned, he saw *One like the Son of Man*. 'When I saw Him, I fell at His feet as though dead'. Then the Lord laid His right hand upon John and said 'Fear not, I am the first and the last ... write the things which thou hast seen and the things which are, and the things which shall be hereafter.'

One of the things which our Lord commanded John to write gives a most glorious promise, and informs us that He *stands at the door* of the human heart, ready to manifest Himself even to lukewarm Laodiceans; and that, if any man hears His voice and *opens the door* (that is, if people are made conscious of their need of Him, so as to open their hearts by the prayer of faith) *He will come in,* feast that one with His gracious presence, and give the delicious fruits of His blessed Spirit. Therefore, the most extraordinary of all of the revelations of Christ (which is that of John in Patmos) shows not only that manifestations run parallel to the canon of Scripture, but also it provides a confirmation of the ordinary revelations of Christ, for which I contend.

Having thus led you from Genesis to Revelation, I conclude by two inferences, which appear to me to be undeniable. The first is that it is evident that our Lord, before His Incarnation, during His stay on earth, and after His Ascension into heaven, has been pleased (in a variety of ways) to manifest Himself to the children of men, both for the benefit of the church in general, for the conversion of sinners, and for the establishment of particular saints.

The second inference is that the doctrine I maintain is as old as Adam, as modern as John (the last of the inspired writers) and as scriptural as the Old and New Testaments, which is what I wanted to demonstrate!

I am convinced that the Lord Jesus Christ, for purposes which are worthy of His wisdom, manifests Himself in this life, to all of His sincere followers, sooner or later.

An Appreciation of John Fletcher

by DAVID RUSHWORTH-SMITH

I believe that it was in the providence of God that my early years in the Christian life were spent amongst the Methodists. For, although I now consider that some of their doctrines are not altogether biblical, my soul derived vast benefit from the things I learned in their midst. Upon reflection, I think it likely that I gained more insight from those Methodists who departed this life many decades previously than from those still alive; it is also true that it took me many months to shake off the liberal theology with which modern Methodism impregnated me; nevertheless, my present attitude towards prayer and evangelism owes much to the things which the Methodists taught me.

It was whilst I read John Wesley's Journal in 1949 that I first began to be attracted to Fletcher of Madeley. I was brought face-to-face repeatedly with comments upon the manner of life of this remarkable person, and enheartened by delightful stories concerning his unique ministry. In fact, John Wesley made me feel that the eighteenth century owed more to John Fletcher than many people realised. Here was a man who had been forgotten by modern christendom, and deprived of mention by the historians, but who appears to have changed the course of national events through his prayers and zeal. It struck me as being strange that such a saint, although reserved (and thus elusive), should be neglected by us if he had been such a source of inspiration and godliness then. The fortunes of history are beyond human explanation, and sometimes the very ones who ought to be long-remembered are pushed out of the limelight by those who have more voluble supporters.

John Fletcher, therefore, began to make a deep impression upon this young lad, although at no small distance, and became the subject of several illustrations in the first sermon that I preached in public, in a little chapel at Seacroft in Yorkshire, on the subject of personal prayer. Stories from his life have cropped up regularly in my sermons from that day to this.

The century into which Fletcher was born, was far from calm; it could be better described as turbulent. This resulted in him being forced to endure much persecution at the hand of heathen forces then reigning in England. However, despite the opposition which he met—and this was considerable—he maintained a Christlike devotion to truth and a calm compassion for others. These noble virtues enabled him both to endure hardship and to win the battle for the Christian faith in the township of Madeley in Shropshire—the only parish in which he served as the appointed minister.

Born in Switzerland in 1729, and educated in that country, Monsieur de la Fléchère—for this was his original name—showed a zeal for the things of God from his earliest years. He was one of those young men who have no fear of being thought religious. Upon his arrival in England in 1750, contact was quickly made with those of like mind. Soon, in St. Albans—as though by chance—he met a born-again lady who so encouraged him to seek a lasting experience of Christ that he made it a matter of the utmost importance to join the misunderstood Methodists. There is little doubt that the doctrinal beliefs of the Christians in his homeland fashioned his views of human life and death. Nevertheless, the company of the two Wesley brothers and George Whitefield, provided the basis for the kind of longing which he had always had afterwards, for an increasingly deep knowledge of the Saviour. His view of salvation was almost calvinistic (if judged by today's standards), but he resolved to have fellowship with the arminian group, although he knew that these people had their failings. Perhaps he had met too much dead orthodoxy to permit him to move freely amongst those who were loud in their claim to eternal life but showed little of it in their homes; there is no doubt that he took every opportunity to denounce unethical behaviour in Christians.

Straight after his ordination in March 1757, this likeable young man—not yet thirty years of age—offered himself to John Wesley as an itinerant colleague. This came in direct answer to prayer and caused the Wesleys ever to have a large place in their hearts for him; his energy, charm, forthrightness, and clarity of thought, were a source of encouragement for three busy years.

Then, deciding that the time had come for him to minister from the base of a settled pastorate, he selected little Madeley as his future home. This was not the only church which was open to him (although it had become obvious that the Bishop of London did not want him in that diocese!), but it was the one which looked as if it would make the most demands of a vicar, and yet offer the least financial reward. For twenty-five years, from 1760, Fletcher laboured here; hated, loved, cursed, adored, persecuted, and misunderstood, he shared the plight of the common people with remarkable patience. Although there were large, well-attended churches in those days, which offered fine stipends, he sought a community which needed him. The love of material things, which looms so large in the twentieth century, was not unknown to this well-brought-up cleric, but the call to deny one's self daily was more

real to him. Such single-mindedness in derelict congregations (for this is an apt description of the situation at
Madeley when he arrived on the scene) can only bring
about either utter failure or complete victory; it pleased
God to revive His work in that pathetic corner of His
vineyard.

During the first year there, this new bachelor vicar knew
abject loneliness, and saw very few folk attend the services.
However, believing that the Lord would have him to be
faithful, even if only one parishioner turned up, he pressed
on. These were days of depression; for weeks on end he
would wrestle with the question 'Am I in God's will?'
Knowing how illogical it was for him to pay heed to the
doubts which crowded in upon him, he could only per-
severe in the face of heavy odds. Finally, after months of
serious prayer and the smallest sign of blessing, he came
to see that this was the place where God would have him
be, despite the lack of response.

Madeley was full of profane and ignorant people; this
was an all-too-obvious fact when Fletcher visited the place
prior to his accepting the parish. Any minister, with lower
principles than this zealot, would be careful how he mentioned such matters from the pulpit. John Fletcher did
not cease to preach against the very things that were daily
joys for the parishioners: drunkenness, orgies, bull-baiting,
and general immorality! We cannot be surprised, therefore, when we read that he suffered many attacks of all
kinds. That his approach was not wrong, however, can be
gained from the fact that—within two years—Madeley had
changed perceptively. What had been a small country
town in which no inhabitant desired decency, and where
all forms of religion were derided, became a holy place;
the church was packed for worship every Sunday, both
morning and evening. We can only presume that his
preaching did not amount to mere denunciations, and that

87

much prayer attended the ministry of the Word. Like Richard Baxter of Kidderminster, and others, John Fletcher found the secret of success in pastoral work.

His prescription for this success appears to have been a mixture of prevailing prayer, personal devotion to the Person of Christ, intensive study of the Scriptures, social concern for the flock, and a willing readiness to visit anyone who was in any form of trouble. He had a special corner in his study which he favoured as a place to pray; there he knelt for hours every day—the wall opposite bearing the mark of his agonised petitions. For two evenings a week he sat up reading, in order to obtain a better understanding of the Christian faith, until—just before dawn and overcome with sleep—he retired for a few hours. He organised, and himself played a large part in, care for the aged, the poor, the dying, widows and orphans. He showed a typical evangelical compassion for the social needs of those around him, and gave sacrificially in order that his vision might become reality. His giving was so extensive that little was left of his stipend for the maintenance of his house and for meals.

I recall one little story which illustrates the power of the divine blessing abounding at Madeley during his ministry: a lady who had been converted, and who wished to be at most of the meetings, suffered from an antagonistic husband. This man was a thorough heathen and did everything that he could in order to keep his wife at home; he went out of his way to make her life a misery. One day, as she put on her coat to go to church, he told her—with obvious sincerity—that he could stand no more of this religion of hers and that unless she stayed at home with him this evening, he would strangle her that night; notwithstanding this threat, the lady set off and joined the congregation. As the time passed, she became fearful, thinking of the reception she would have upon her return

88

home. Mr. Fletcher, who knew nothing of this incident, was finding the service heavy going. He did not preach from notes usually, relying upon his memory and the Holy Spirit to bring his thorough preparation to mind, as he spoke. This particular evening, he could not remember his points or even the general outline of the message. Feeling downcast about this unusual situation, and unwilling to speak without inward assurance, he determined to make do with Bible readings only. However, suddenly, he found that his mind was filling with thoughts upon quite a different subject. Deciding that the Lord was working things together for the good of someone, he shared his anxiety with the gathered flock, then plunged into this new sermon. He did not realise what he was doing until the next day, but for half-an-hour he encouraged this worried woman from the story of the fiery furnace in Daniel! Now unafraid, the wife hurried back to the waiting husband, assured that no harm would come to her. What met her eyes, however, was beyond her wildest dreams; her heathen man was down on the floor, face to the boards, in an agony of religious conviction, crying out to God for mercy!

Eight years after his induction at Madeley, the Countess of Huntingdon asked Mr. Fletcher to become the president of her newly founded college for student ministers. This was no small honour since there were other clergymen who were better known to this titled lady, and who more fully shared her theological point of view. However, all forms of earthly honour seem to have been of little value to this exceptional man; he did not consider anything from merely a human standpoint. He refused to accept this office, unless it could be a part-time appointment; he wished to remain the vicar of Madeley and continue in the pastoral office. Knowing how easy it is for any minister to run away from the problems of church life by escaping into the quieter confines of a teaching career, I admire this particular stand of Fletcher. It would have been understandable if he had accepted this post and put his church in the care of another. Eight years of hard work are a good reason for some years of lighter duties. This kind of logic made no sense to this high-minded man of God; promotion and easy living had no attraction at all; he knew that he must be down amongst the people. In fact, later on, when the king pressed him to accept a high clerical office in London, he replied—somewhat succinctly— that he wished for nothing but more grace!

The countess, faced with a choice between either Fletcher's terms of acceptance or not having him as the college president, surrendered to his precise offer. She could not have known what a season of blessing there was to follow this appointment. The students confessed that they did not know, at times, if they were in this world or the next. For days at a time, they spent long hours doing nothing other than seeking the face of the Saviour. On occasions, they would not refer to their study books at all for a whole week. The visits of the college president were times of pentecostal visitation; voluntary confession, heart-searching, and delightful prayer meetings, were the natural order of the day. This behaviour might seem strange to those who know that John Fletcher was such an opponent of extremism and so voluble a contender for the need of each minister to be both a student and a man acquainted with contemporary events. Considering that the college was well furnished with competent teachers, Fletcher took the line that he was a sort of visiting pastor who ought to stir up the ordinands in their faith. Knowing the practical problems which they would meet in parish life, he considered that they had need of the most intimate knowledge of the Son of God. He urged them all to seek God in order that they might become partakers of the divine promises, and living emblems of the power of the Almighty.

During this period in his life, he would sometimes be away from his own pulpit on Sundays. Arrangements were made for some of Wesley's itinerant preachers to take his place. Although they were not so eloquent, or as well bred as himself, and despite the fact that his people now wished for none but their own minister to lead the worship, he told his congregation that they would do well to hear more acceptable preachers than himself, when occasion permitted! Unlike so many who refuse to vacate their pulpits, for fear that a better man might occupy the same during their absence, Fletcher considered every other preacher—however unlearned—to be better than himself.

The spiritual refreshment which shook Trevecca College continuously during this presidency would doubtless have remained if there had not been a bitter controversy within the ranks of the Methodist societies. Although this theological division had been boiling up for several years, it was not until 1770 that open ferment was seen. It is easy for us now to see that lack of wisdom, ungracious spirits, ready tempers, and unfortunate grammar, were the real culprits behind the whole affair. In the heat of the differences, such calm diagnosis was almost impossible. John Fletcher did his best to repair the breach and heal the wounds; his labours, though praised by all concerned, were of no avail; minds had been made up and there was an unattractive, unrelenting spirit abroad. Fletcher found himself on the other side of the controversy from the Countess of Huntingdon and felt obliged to resign. This was a sad moment for him, and a shock from which the college hardly recovered; however, it was a matter of principle, and the resignation could not be avoided. His flock at Madeley received the news with as much joy as the students at Trevecca greeted it with tears.

John Fletcher was unwilling to pronounce upon a matter until he was sure of the facts. When he had fully assured himself as to the truth concerning something, he could be relied upon to blazon it abroad. Such zeal, added to his natural abilities, caused him to become a prolific writer. As a result of this, we are still able to see how graciously a man can speak of his opponents and of heretics. All of his pamphlets, booklets, sermons, and theses, are written with invincible charity and the noblest courtesy; his outspoken attacks upon the main heresies of his day (including unitarianism) were masterpieces of clarity, truth and uncommon affection for the souls of those enmeshed in lies. Instead of making his theological enemies feel small (which is the trait of this century), he made them feel wanted by his Saviour. This approach made more than a few stalwarts of untruth seek to understand the Scriptures better. I consider it most unfortunate that his work is not better read than it is. Modern controversies might die quicker if the Christian personalities involved had Fletcher's example to lean on.

His unchanging attitude towards money and every form of worldly wealth, must have appeared incomprehensible to his contemporaries; he was quite unmoved by offers of comfort and luxuries. In fact, purely on the grounds of the fact that a 'certain young lady' had wealth, he spurned the love of the one woman he felt he could marry. Only after Miss Bosanquet had been disowned by her family for her evangelical views, which was twenty-five years after they first met, did Fletcher break his silence and make the long-awaited proposal. Even then, he made it quite clear that, although he loved her, it was her penury which made it possible for him to approach her in this way!

They were married in 1781, when the groom was fifty-two years old. It was a blissful enterprise and accepted gloriously in Madeley, even though the bride was a native of Leytonstone and not a local girl. It seems sad that such a happy partnership was broken forcibly by death only three years and nine months later.

Throughout the whole of the ministerial life of John Fletcher, he knew remarkable spiritual power in preaching; there is little doubt that he was anointed with divine unction and spoke in the demonstration of the Holy Spirit. His regular congregation grew by leaps and bounds, the young and the old being greatly affected at every service; tears were commonplace. It did not matter where he went in the British Isles, nor the language spoken by the people, the result was the same; on the continent, as in his parish, whole audiences were reduced to a state of deep conviction. Sometimes the congregations could not disperse for hours after his preaching was finished, because of the mutual longing for divine grace to follow repentance.

So powerful, and so eloquent a preacher was Fletcher that John Wesley affirmed repeatedly that it was he, and not George Whitefield, who should have such national fame. Wesley did not say this spitefully, for he had the highest regard for his ardent colleague Whitefield; he was looking at the facts in a logical way, and gave his own opinion. In fact, Wesley went further and placed upon record his constant wish that Fletcher be made the leader of the Methodist movement, after his death. Little did he know then, that he would outlive his colleague by six years, despite the difference in their ages.

Fletcher's ministry, with its powerful effect upon the populace, caused jealousy to rise in his relationships with neighbouring clergy. Their reaction to the divine blessing at Madeley was not to praise God for the change, nor to thank Fletcher for bringing a new spirit into the area; they criticised the unwanted minister. They got together and made an official complaint about him on the grounds of schism. Their argument was that his regular recommendation for good living so upset some of the communicants at Madeley that they could not bear to attend the communion services. Since these folk were, by virtue of their baptism, members of the local church, and since the vicar had caused them to stop making their communion by his preaching, therefore he was dividing the Body of Christ!

Fletcher found that it was pointless trying to argue with people about spiritual matters if they were not born-again; he did not try to convince them that he was right, therefore, by tirades and letters of self-justification, he meekly bore the persecution. What letters he wrote, by way of reply to the offensive missives he received, were the warmest of communications. In due course, his enemies learned to respect his godly attitude towards all things.

Sometimes his preaching would contain prophetic utterances of apostolic quality. On one occasion he turned aside from his message to foretell—with great accuracy—the French Revolution; this long-drawn-out terror did not begin to take place until four years after his death. On other occasions, he would—without warning—begin to lay hold of God for the healing of a parishioner. Although he appears to have done this only when led of God to do so, and although he was careful not to pray for the healing of others until he had first made them aware of the whole content of the Gospel, there are many cases of remarkable healing on record. However, despite these results, it could not be said that he was some kind of *healing evangelist*; he did not *offer* healing, or salvation, as though he were the purveyor of such blessing.

When it was discovered that he was suffering from tuberculosis, he remained as calm as ever, asserting—with child-like simplicity—that he was in need of divine chastisement. Instead of resting or playing the role of patient, he went on a preaching tour to Switzerland in order to share with his fellow countrymen the things which God had shown him in recent years. He bore suffering in the same way that he endured misunderstanding; despite his sensitive nature, he was able—by God's help—to remain calm in every crisis.

His death in 1785, at the age of fifty-five, was untimely and premature; he had lived like a flame of fire but had burned out more quickly than was expected; the whole country was saddened by the loss. John Wesley promised to write his life story as soon as he could accomplish it, so that this man's experiences might be set down for posterity. A year later, at the age of eighty-three, the task was complete. In that large manuscript Wesley wrote 'I have not known one so uniformly and deeply devoted to God ... nor do I expect to find another such, on this side of eternity.'

If he had lived a little longer he would have been the prime mover in the foundation of an official Methodist Church. Any kind of splits in church fellowship were abhorrent to him, yet he had written at length, as early as 1775, that division between the Anglicans and Methodists would become necessary. This does not mean that he adopted secessionist ideals pointlessly, nor that he refused to see any other viewpoint; it means that he came to see the need for either a complete reformation of the state church, with resultant revised prayer book and doctrines, or else a separate evangelical body. He was ahead of his time in this respect as in others; such suggestions as these, when he made them in one of his many manuscripts, were quite unacceptable. However, the time came when the break was forced upon the Methodists by circumstances. This resulted in a shambles of divisions and splits which would have broken Fletcher's heart. If such action is ever necessary, it should be based upon the kind of scriptural principles which he advocated; schism based upon precipitate decision or environments must lead to difficulties afterwards. It is unfortunate that his colleagues did not pay more heed to Fletcher whilst they had time to do so. They would have saved themselves much trouble by taking note of his wise counsel.

It is my opinion that believers of today would suffer no loss if they had the same charity, graciousness, and clarity of thought that were the daily companions of the Reverend John Fletcher. I hope that this book will have whetted the appetite of the reader to obtain a copy of the life story of this remarkable man,[1] and to read further literary efforts from this sanctified pen.

In December 1968, David Rushworth-Smith gave a lecture on John Fletcher at the Westminster Conference in London. Copies of that lecture are still available from Christian Bookshops. It is titled 'John Fletcher'.